a year
in your garden

a year
in your garden

JANE COURTIER

This is a Parragon Publishing Book
First published in 2002

Parragon Publishing
Queen Street House
4 Queen Street
Bath BA1 1HE, UK

Created and produced by The Bridgewater Book Company Ltd.

ISBN: 0-75259-709-4

Printed in China

NOTE
For growing and harvesting, calendar information applies
only to the Northern Hemisphere (US zones 5–9).

contents

introduction

Gardening is a captivating hobby and a year-through pastime for millions of people. During spring and summer the weather and light encourage daily visits to gardens, perhaps to inspect and admire a special plant that has just come into flower. In winter, however, the reduction in the hours of daylight means that for many people gardening is only possible at weekends. But whatever the size of

▼ *The pleasures of the summer garden are intensified by the gentle sound of splashing water from a garden pool.*

your garden and the time of year, there is always something to be done, even if it is just to remove dead leaves from around a much treasured alpine plant. During summer even the smallest patio or courtyard garden benefits from the regular removal of dead flowers from window boxes, hanging baskets, and tubs. Shrubs often need yearly pruning, while many herbaceous plants require staking and deadheading; half-hardy annuals are sown in gentle warmth in greenhouses and conservatories in late winter and early spring, and hardy annuals directly

into borders in mid- and late spring. The routine of gardening tasks continues and lawns need regular attention if an attractive and healthy sward is to be created throughout summer.

Digging the soil and preparing it for planting and sowing are other regular jobs, together with the continuing necessity to pull up and hoe off weeds. If left, they compete with cultivated plants for space and food.

All of these tasks have a season, and within this all-color book there are reminders and advice about what to do.

◄ Freesia corms must be planted in late summer if you are to enjoy their scented blooms during the winter months.

▼ With a little forward planning, containers can provide color and interest for the patio virtually the whole year round.

The gardening year divides into four well known seasons—spring, summer, fall, and winter—and these can be further divided into early, mid-, and late seasons. This broadly equates to the months of the year but exactly when these fall depends on the climate in your area. Early summer is usually June, with mid-summer assumed to be July and late summer as August. But even within the relatively short distance of five hundred miles spring can be delayed by three to four weeks, and in cold areas autumn and winter will come earlier than in mild regions. If you are new to gardening—or have taken over an existing garden—during the first few years carefully note when you sow seeds or set out plants into borders, so that if a frost cuts down young plants in spring you will know to perform the job slightly later during the following year. The flowering times of shrubs and trees will also be influenced by the weather

and keeping a record of these will help to widen your interest in gardening.

Changing times

For many people the whole nature of gardening has changed during recent decades. Jobs that were once physically demanding are now much easier to tackle by using powered tools, from electrically-driven lawn mowers to hedge clippers and chainsaws. Demands on personal leisure time have increased and many gardeners are now looking for convenience gardening where color is quickly produced and lasts over a long period. Garden centers and nurseries sell plants in containers which are ready for planting out and this, too, has inspired and continued this change. Gardening is both a participatory and spectator pastime; we are active in our own gardens throughout the year as well as regularly taking the opportunity to visit the many splendid and inspirational

gardens that are open throughout most seasons. Also, there is an opportunity to view local gardens as they are passed. They all offer ideas about ways to use plants in gardens; do not rely on your memory, jot down notes of them in a book.

the garden in spring

Spring is a wonderful season for gardeners, a time of rebirth when winter casts off its gloom and plants burst into growth. Day-by-day we can see gardens coming into life. Fresh shoots appear on plants, with young leaves unfolding and an abundance of flowers revealing a rich tapestry of color. Spring is the time to get to work in a garden and, although a busy one, it is possibly the most exciting season of the year.

early spring

Ever-lengthening days give us more time to spend in the garden and we need it because there is plenty to be done. Although the days are still chilly, with overnight frost an ever-present danger, there is more sunshine to cheer things up, and a distinctly milder feel to the air.

Better weather, spring sunshine, and the obvious signs of growth and flowering around the garden make everyone feel optimistic and enthusiastic, but it pays to be cautious for a little while yet. In many places, reliably warm weather is still some weeks away and a late frost can still occur.

Most gardeners will be hoping for several days of dry, sunny weather, preferably accompanied by a good strong breeze: ideal conditions for drying out the soil ready for seedbed preparation. The lighter the soil, the earlier this task can be done. It just involves raking the surface until the soil is reduced to an even texture of fine crumbs, but it's essential to wait until the soil is no longer clinging and sticky.

Although the spring may seem slow to get going, it soon moves up a gear and suddenly gardeners are hard pushed to keep up. There are spring bulbs to support and deadhead, border plants to stake before they start to flop over, containers to get ready for the summer display, and sowings to make both outdoors and inside. There's also planting and pruning to be done, and dozens of seedlings jostling for space in the greenhouse. In fact sometimes it's so busy that there hardly seems time to enjoy the garden itself. So whatever else you do, make time to appreciate that delicious freshness of growth the garden offers now, for there's no other season quite like it.

◀ *As the days gradually become brighter and warmer, eagerly awaited spring flowers surge into growth.*

EARLY SPRING TASKS

General
- Prepare the soil for sowing when the weather allows
- Remove weeds and apply a moisture-retaining mulch

Ornamental garden
- Plant container-grown trees and shrubs, and plant and divide herbaceous perennials
- Support border plants as soon as the shoots start to lengthen

- Sow hardy annuals and Lathyrus odoratus (sweet peas) outdoors
- Prune roses and shrubs such as buddleja, hydrangeas, and Cornus alba (dogwood)
- Remove winter protection from tender plants

- Fertilize spring-flowering bulbs, perennials, and shrubs if not already done
- Mulch round alpine plants with fresh gravel
- Trim back winter-flowering calluna (heathers)

▼ A fresh dressing of gravel around alpine plants helps to show the developing flowers off to perfection.

Lawns
- Begin mowing regularly; continue to carry out repairs to turf

Kitchen garden
- Dig up the last of the overwintered crops and sow early crops in their place
- Plant early potatoes, rhubarb, and shallots

- Continue harvesting rhubarb and kale
- Stake fall- or early spring-sown fava beans and peas

- Protect early blossom on fruit trees
- Plant soft-fruit bushes
- Check raspberry supports

Greenhouse
- Keep the glass clean for good light transmission
- Sow half-hardy annuals, herbs, and eggplant, cucumbers, sweet peppers, and tomatoes; prick off seedlings sown earlier
- Start chrysanthemums and dahlias into growth to produce cuttings if not already done
- Take softwood cuttings of overwintered plants started into growth earlier

- Ventilate the greenhouse with care; if possible fit an automatic ventilator to allow a quick response to sudden temperature changes
- Plant tuberous begonias
- Check plants regularly for pests and diseases
- Buy growing bags for tomatoes and other greenhouse crops, and allow them to warm up in the greenhouse

- Store left-over seeds in a cool, dry place
- Repot greenhouse and houseplants as necessary
- Plant out forced bulbs in the garden when they have finished flowering

▼ The greenhouse will soon be filling with softwood cuttings from a range of overwintered plants.

plants in season

Day by day, more fresh young leaves and flowers fill the garden, bringing it alive after its long dormant period. Bulbs are among the most prominent plants, but there are many shrubs, trees, and perennials now putting on a tremendous performance.

▼ The luscious purple flowers of aubrieta will brighten up any garden at this time of year.

PERENNIALS AND BEDDING PLANTS

Aubrieta
Bergenia cordifolia
Doronicum (leopard's bane)
Primula vulgaris, and others (primrose)
Pulmonaria (lungwort)

BULBS

Anemone (windflower)
Bulbocodium vernum
Chionodoxa (glory of the snow)
Crocus
Cyclamen coum
Eranthis (winter aconite)
Erythronium (dog's tooth violet)
Iris danfordiae, I. reticulata
Leucojum vernum (snowflake)
Muscari (grape hyacinth)
Narcissus (daffodil)
Pushkinia scilloides
Tulipa kaufmanniana, T. fosteriana,
    T. tarda, and others (tulip)

▲ 'Dark Secret', an early-flowering tulip,
is a new cultivar with luscious deep colors
that will bring warmth to any garden.

TREES AND SHRUBS

Acer pseudoplatanus 'Brilliantissimum'
    (sycamore), A. rubrum (red maple)
Calluna 'Spring Cream', C. 'Spring Torch',
    and others (heather)
Camellia japonica (common camellia)
Chaenomeles speciosa, C. japonica (japonica)
Chimonanthus praecox (wintersweet)
Clematis armandii
Cornus mas (cornelian cherry)
Corylopsis pauciflora (winter hazel)
Erica carnea varieties (winter heath)
Forsythia intermedia, F. suspensa
Magnolia stellata (star magnolia)
Prunus cerasifera pissardii (cherry plum)
Salix caprea (willow)

▶ The cheerful pink and white flowers of
Anemone blanda are happy in light shade as
well as full sun. Blue forms are also available.

planting and sowing

It is time for most gardeners to start sowing in earnest at last, although gardeners with heavy soils or gardens in particularly cold, exposed positions may be better advised to hang on just a little while longer. Always garden according to the prevailing conditions rather than calendar dates.

Prepare the soil for sowing

Soil in a seedbed should be broken down to fine, even crumbs, usually known as "a fine tilth." If the soil is left in large clods it is very difficult to get a level seedbed, and seeds will end up being buried either too deeply or too shallowly to achieve successful germination.

If the vegetable garden has been left roughly dug over the winter months, frosts will have got at the clods of soil, breaking them up by the action of repeated freezing and thawing.

As soon as a spell of dry, breezy weather has dried out the soil surface sufficiently, these clods can be reduced to fine crumbs by raking. Any particularly large clods can usually be broken down easily by a smart blow with the back of the rake.

BEGIN SOWING VEGETABLE CROPS

Some time during early spring, depending on the weather, a wide range of vegetables can be sown, including beans, carrots, leeks, lettuces, parsnips, summer and fall cabbages, early summer cauliflowers, spinach, and Swiss chard. Draw straight drills using a garden line and a hoe, and sow the seeds thinly along the drill. Rake the soil carefully over the seeds, tamp it down lightly, and label the row clearly. It is too early for the more tender crops such as zucchini, marrows, and bush and pole beans to be sown outside, but they can be raised in pots in a greenhouse for planting out after the last frost.

▲ *A light touch with the rake is necessary in order to produce a fine, even surface to a seedbed. Large stones should be removed.*

plant potatoes

If growing space is limited, plant early potatoes rather than main crops, choosing some of the more uncommon varieties that are impossible to buy from the store. The earliest crops of new potatoes have an incomparable flavor when they are freshly lifted. The foliage of potatoes is sensitive to frost, so take care about the planting time. It generally takes two or three weeks before the shoots show through the soil after planting.

1 As an alternative to immediate planting, seed potatoes can be set on a cool, light windowsill to produce shoots (below). The eyes that produce the shoots are clustered together at one end of the tuber (the "rose" end), and tubers should be set in egg cartons with this end uppermost.

2 Potatoes should be planted in well-prepared soil, in rows 18in/45cm apart, and spaced 12–18in/30–45cm apart within the row (below). Sprouted (or "chitted") tubers will appear through the soil more quickly after planting, but they need to be handled carefully in order to avoid knocking the shoots off.

3 Draw wide drills using a draw hoe, or use a trowel to make individual planting holes. Plant the potatoes around 5in/13cm deep. Chitted tubers should be put carefully into the holes with the shoots at the top as they are very fragile and easily broken. Unsprouted tubers should be planted with the rose end facing up.

4 Check the rows of potatoes regularly to see when the first shoots appear; they are dark bluish-green (right). Be on your guard against frost. If an unexpected frost kills the first shoots all is not lost—new shoots should replace them.

◀ *Most gardens have room for some soft fruit. Early spring is a good time to plant container-grown bushes and canes.*

mid-spring

The garden really is looking good now, with the trees clothed in fresh young leaves, lawns becoming a richer green, and spring flowers at their peak. A little warm, sunny weather brings out a real enthusiasm for gardening and there's certainly plenty to keep the keenest gardener occupied.

▲ *Tulips and forget-me-nots make a classic combination in the spring garden. Next year's spring bedding will need to be sown soon.*

Gardeners are not the only ones who are enjoying the spring weather, and pests and weeds are now thriving. Weeding is a job that needs to be done for a large proportion of the year, but weeds are probably growing most rapidly in mid-spring. It's especially important to keep them under control while garden plants are small because they can easily be smothered by weed growth.

Pests, too, are on the increase, attracted by the tender young growth the plants are making. Slugs and snails are often a particular problem, and aphids (greenfly) can be found clustered on shoot tips, especially on greenhouse plants. Early action helps to prevent an outbreak turning into an epidemic which will be hard to control.

There may be some slightly tender plants that appear to have been killed by the winter cold, but don't consign them to the compost pile. It is sometimes well into the summer before they show signs of recovery and start to put out buds. Check by gently scraping a little patch of bark from the main stem—if the wood underneath is green and moist, the plant is still alive.

Spring bulbs continue to make a stunning show; wherever possible they should be deadheaded as they fade, before they have a chance to set seed.

Spring bedding plants are also putting on a good performance; make a note to obtain more seeds of plants such as *Erysimum* (wallflowers), *Bellis perennis*, (daisies), *Myosotis*, (forget-me-nots) and so on, so they are not overlooked when they need to be sown in early summer. Buy the seeds when you buy summer bedding plants from the garden center.

There's plenty to do in the kitchen garden in mid-spring, too, with weeding, sowing, and planting out, plus thinning out of crops that have been sown earlier.

In the greenhouse, shading becomes necessary soon, and ventilation and watering should be increased as the weather grows warmer and sunnier.

MID-SPRING TASKS

General
- Control weeds, slugs, snails, and other pests as they appear
- Check plants that appear to have been killed by frosts

Ornamental garden
- Plant summer-flowering bulbs and deadhead spring bulbs. Buy bedding plants from garden centers
- Continue to sow hardy annuals
- Take cuttings of border plants
- Plant galanthus (snowdrops) "in the green" (while in leaf)
- Check for reverted shoots on variegated shrubs
- Check for rose diseases and treat as necessary
- Plant alpines and evergreens
- Prune spring-flowering shrubs such as forsythia after flowering

▼ Neatly trimmed edges set off a freshly mown lawn.

Lawns
- Apply a "weed and feed" combined herbicide and fertilizer
- Mow and edge lawns as necessary
- Deal with worm casts and moss
- Make new lawns from seed

Water garden
- Begin excavation work for a new pond

Kitchen garden
- Continue sowing successional crops. Prepare the trench for pole beans
- Sow winter brassicas outdoors
- Hoe off weeds regularly
- Plant out leeks and onion sets
- Earth up potatoes and plant second early and maincrop varieties
- Spray fruit with fungicide if mildew has been a problem in previous years
- Avoid spraying fruit trees with insecticides while pollinating insects are active
- Prune plums

▼ Seedlings and young plants continue to need potting up and pricking off in the greenhouse.

Greenhouse
- Apply shading and increase ventilation and watering
- Check heaters are still working
- Begin hardening off bedding plants
- Continue pricking off and potting up as necessary
- Plant out tomatoes in the greenhouse border
- Sow pole and bush beans, and melons

plants in season

Many shrubs and trees join the throng of flowering plants in mid-spring, and increasing numbers of border plants are producing their blooms now, too. The earliest of the spring bulbs are over, but there are still plenty providing a good show of color.

▼ *Most euphorbias brighten spring with their lime-green flowerheads, but the steely blue leaves often persist right through the winter, too.*

TREES AND SHRUBS

Acer pseudoplatanus 'Brilliantissimum'
    (sycamore), *A. rubrum* (red maple)
Amelanchier lamarckii (juneberry)
Berberis darwinii, B. stenophylla (barberry)
Ceanothus (California lilac)
Clematis alpina, C. armandii
Cytisus praecox (broom)
Daphne burkwoodii, D. cneorum
Forsythia
Kerria japonica
Magnolia × *soulangiana, M. stellata*
    (star magnolia)
Malus (apple, crab apple)
Osmanthus burkwoodii, O. delavayii
Pieris
Prunus in variety (ornamental cherry)
Rhododendron
Ribes sanguineum (flowering currant)
Rosmarinus officinalis (rosemary)
Spiraea arguta (bridal wreath)
Ulex europaeus (furze)
Vinca major (greater periwinkle), *V. minor*
    (lesser periwinkle)

▲ *The stately chalices of* Magnolia ×
soulangiana *blooms are often spoiled
by late frosts in exposed positions.*

▼ *The flowering currant,* Ribes sanguineum, *is
an easily pleased shrub with attractive rosy
flowers and a pungent aroma to the foliage.*

PERENNIALS AND BEDDING PLANTS

Aurinia saxatilis
Aubrieta
Bellis perennis (common daisy)
Bergenia
Erysimum cheirii (wallflower)
Doronicum (leopard's bane)
Epimedium (barrenwort)
Euphorbia characias, E. polychroma
Helleborus orientalis (lenten rose)
Iberis sempervirens (candytuft)
Myosotis (forget-me-not)
Primula (primrose)

BULBS

Anemone
Bulbocodium vernum
Chionodoxa (glory of the snow)
Convallaria majalis (lily-of-the-valley)
Eythronium revolutum (American trout lily)
Fritillaria imperialis (crown imperial),
    F. meleagris (snake's head fritillary)
Leucojum vernum (spiking snowflake)
Muscari (grape hyacinth)
Narcissus (daffodil)
Tulipa (tulip)

lawns

The lawn is an integral part of the garden, providing a restful green backdrop against which to admire the vibrant colors of the flowers. Lawns that may have looked tired and thin after the stress of the winter should now be growing more strongly, and it's time to help them reach perfection.

Apply lawn fertilizer

In spring, a fertilizer containing high levels of nitrogen applied to a lawn will boost growth and help the grass to develop a rich green color. The phosphates and potash also included in lawn fertilizers stimulate root growth and improve resistance to disease and adverse weather conditions.

▼ *Mid-spring is an ideal time to make a new lawn from seed. Sow in soil that has been carefully prepared to create a fine tilth.*

Fertilizers are available as powders, granules, or liquids. Liquid fertilizers can be applied with a hose-end dilutor; they are fast acting and give a rapid response, but they can be expensive for large lawns. Dry fertilizers can be applied by hand but it is very difficult to achieve an even distribution, and the result can be patchy. The best method is to use a fertilizer distributor, a small hopper on wheels that applies the fertilizer at a given rate when pushed up and down

the lawn. Take care to cover all the grass evenly, and do not overlap strips or leave a gap between them because this will show up as differently colored growth later on.

CONTROL LAWN WEEDS

Where there are only a few, isolated weeds in the lawn they can be treated individually, either by digging them out with a narrow-bladed trowel or special lawn-

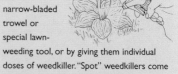

weeding tool, or by giving them individual doses of weedkiller. "Spot" weedkillers come in the form of wax sticks, impregnated sponges, aerosols and ready-to-use sprays. If weeds are more widespread over the lawn surface, an overall application of selective weedkiller is necessary. This should be applied shortly after fertilizing, or you can use a proprietary "weed and feed" product that applies the two together. Be very careful not to allow lawn weedkillers to drift on to cultivated plants or neighboring gardens. Tiny amounts carried on the breeze are enough to do a great deal of damage to other plants.

► *Grass seed should germinate rapidly in warm, moist, spring weather. This is a good time to repair worn patches by oversowing them.*

mow and edge lawns

A perfect, velvet-textured, emerald-green lawn is the envy of all who see it, but many gardeners seem to find it impossible to achieve. Understanding and employing the correct mowing technique is one simple way to greatly improve the quality of the turf.

1 Now the grass has started to grow rapidly it will need cutting more frequently—once a week at least, and twice a week as spring moves into summer. Before mowing, clear stones, fir cones, sticks, and other debris from the lawn. If you can, wait until the dew has dried.

2 Set the blades at the right height (right); scalping is a very common mistake. At this time of year the grass should be left between ¾in/18mm and 1¼in/30mm high, reducing to a minimum of ½in/12mm high in summer (¾in/18mm is better for most lawns).

3 Mow the grass in parallel strips up and down the lawn (above). If the mower has a rear roller it will produce the light and dark stripes favored by many people; in this case it is important to keep the mowing strips as straight and even as possible for the best effect.

4 Next time the lawn is mown, work at right angles to the last direction of cut—across the lawn rather than up and down. Alternating the direction at each cut makes sure that the surface of the lawn remains even, and helps control lawn weeds and weed grasses.

5 Once the mowing is finished, trim the edges to give a neat appearance (above). Use long-handled edging shears or, to save time, a powered edger. If the edges are ragged after the winter, recut them in spring with a half-moon edging iron, using a plank as a straight edge.

late spring

The weather is mild and there's often a good deal of sunshine. Spring blossom mingles with the early blooms of summer, and foliage still has a wonderful freshness. Gardeners should enjoy the last weeks of spring while they prepare for summer in what is always one of the year's busiest times.

In most areas, the risk of damaging night frosts will be over toward the end of spring, but in the early days, and in colder regions, you will need to remain on your guard. If your garden happens to be in a frost pocket, you may need to be much more cautious than neighbors only a short distance away who are in a more favored position.

This is a good time to plant up hanging baskets, window boxes, and tubs which are very valuable for injecting concentrated splashes of color into the garden and around the house. They are increasingly popular, with a wide range of new and unusual "patio plants" available at garden centers. Keep them under cover or in a sheltered position for a few days after planting in the early part of the month.

Spring bedding plants are past their best now, and need to be cleared out to make way for the summer bedding—but don't forget to sow spring bedding plants ahead in preparation for next year's display.

Plants are growing strongly in late spring but need to be regularly fed and weeded; pests must be controlled promptly. In the vegetable garden, tender crops such as pole beans, bush beans, and zucchini can be sown safely out of doors.

Finally, if you want to introduce a watery element, a pond is a wonderful addition to any garden, adding a special sort of tranquillity with its shimmering water and colorful plants.

The gentle splash of a fountain or waterfall is an extra delight. This is the best time of year to build a garden pool, and you can rest assured that you are creating a feature that is bound to be enjoyed for many years to come.

▶ *Well-planted containers are particularly useful for adding color to the patio. Wait until frosts are over before putting them outside.*

LATE SPRING TASKS

General

:: Check for pests on plants and treat promptly
:: Feed strong growing plants
:: Treat perennial weeds with herbicide

Ornamental garden

:: Plant up hanging baskets, window boxes, and tubs
:: Continue staking border plants
:: Weed annual seedlings and thin them as necessary
:: Remove spring bedding plants; plant out summer bedding plants

:: Plant dahlias
:: Deadhead narcissus (daffodils). Leave the foliage in place until six weeks after the last flowers fade
:: Sow winter-flowering viola (pansies), and biennials such as erysimum (wallflowers), Dianthus barbatus (Sweet Williams), and myosotis (forget-me-nots)
:: Water recently planted trees and shrubs if the weather is dry
:: Trim evergreen hedges as necessary

▲ *Plant up containers with a range of summer bedding plants for a pleasing display.*

Lawns

:: Lower the height of the mower blades to give a closer cut. Tackle weeds with a spot weedkiller

Water garden

:: Construct and plant up new ponds. Introduce fish once the plants are established
:: In existing ponds, divide deep-water aquatics and plant new varieties
:: Feed fish, but be careful not to overfeed
:: Watch for aphids on water lily leaves, and submerge affected leaves to allow fish to eat them

▼ *Strawing around strawberry plants helps protect the fruit from slug damage and soil splashes.*

Kitchen garden

:: Water as necessary, timing the watering carefully for maximum crops
:: Continue to make successional sowings for continuity of supply
:: Plant out hardened-off pole and bush beans once the risk of frost is over. Sow pole beans and bush beans outdoors

:: Thin out seedlings in the rows. Thin carrots late in the evening to avoid attracting carrot root fly. Stake peas
:: Plant vegetables in pots and growing bags
:: Check plums for silver leaf disease
:: Reduce codling moth damage with pheromone traps

:: Straw around strawberries and net the plants against birds

Greenhouse

:: Ventilate the greenhouse more freely, and water more frequently as the weather gets warmer
:: Train and support cucumbers, melons, and tomatoes

:: Continue pricking off seedlings and potting up rooted cuttings as necessary

:: "Stop" pelargoniums and fuchsias by pinching out the growing points to make them bushier

plants in season

Alpine and rock garden plants will be producing a bright display at this time of year. Wisteria and laburnum are draped with long racemes of blue and yellow flowers respectively. Rhododendrons and azaleas are also strikingly colorful during this month.

▼ *The fragrant flowers of wisteria are often among the most spectacular blooms in the garden in the late spring.*

▲ The glossy, aromatic leaves of Choisya ternata *(Mexican orange blossom)* are a bright lime-green in the variety 'Sundance'.

▼ Ceanothus 'Concha': dense clusters of brilliant, sky-blue flowers make this a popular plant for a sheltered spot.

TREES AND SHRUBS

Aesculus hippocastanum (horse chestnut)
Berberis (barberry)
Buddleja globosa
Ceanothus (Californian lilac)
Cercis siliquastrum (Judas tree)
Choisya ternata (Mexican orange blossom)
Clematis montana and large-flowered hybrids
Crataegus (hawthorn)
Crinodendron hookerianum
Davidia involucrata (handkerchief tree)
Deutzia gracilis, D. rosea
Genista hispanica (Spanish gorse)
Kerria japonica
Kolkwitzia amabilis (beauty bush)
Laburnum
Magnolia × *soulangiana*
Malus (apple, crab apple)
Paeonia (peony)
Pieris
Potentilla fruticosa (cinquefoil)
Prunus (ornamental cherry)
Rhododendron (including azaleas)
Robinia hispida, R. margaretta
Rosmarinus officinalis (rosemary)
Sambucus racemosa plumosa 'Aurea'
    (red-berried elder)
Sorbus aria (whitebeam), *S. aucuparia*
    (mountain ash)
Spiraea arguta (bridal wreath)
Syringa (lilac)
Viburnum opulus (guelder rose),
    V. plicatum (Japanese snowball bush)
Weigela
Wisteria

BULBS

Allium
Anemone (windflower)
Convallaria majalis (lily-of-the-valley)
Fritillaria imperialis (crown imperial)
Hyacinthoides non-scripta (English bluebell)
Hyacinthus (hyacinth)
Leucojum aestivum (summer snowflake)
Tulipa (tulip)

PERENNIALS AND BEDDING PLANTS

Ajuga reptans (bugle)
Aurinia saxatilis (Alyssum saxatile)
    (gold dust)
Aquilegia (columbine)
Armeria (sea pink)
Aubrieta
Dicentra spectabilis (bleeding heart)
Euphorbia (spurge)
Geranium
Helianthemum (rock rose)
Iberis (candytuft)
Lithodora diffusa
Primula (primrose)
Saxifraga umbrosa

planting and sowing

Crops in the kitchen garden are growing apace. If the weather is dry, some are likely to need watering to keep them growing strongly, but it's important to know when to water. It should now be safe to sow pole beans in the open: by the time the seedlings appear, frosts should be a thing of the past.

Sow pole and bush beans outdoors

By late spring the soil should be warm enough for bean seeds to germinate

◄ *Flowers on climbing bean plants sometimes fall without setting pods. This is generally due to dry conditions; watering will cure the problem.*

quickly, and the seedlings should be safe from frosts. Bush beans are sown in single rows, spaced some 3in/7.5cm apart. Climbing beans and pole beans need supports, which are generally put in place before sowing; a double row of bamboo stakes, crossing at the top, works well. High yields have also been obtained from rows of stakes spaced 2ft/60cm apart, with stakes 12in/30cm apart in the row, sowing two seeds at the base of each stake.

There are many varieties of bush and pole beans available. With dwarf bush beans, look for varieties that hold their pods well clear of the ground because this avoids beans being eaten by slugs or spoiled by soil splashes. Purple- or gold-podded varieties are easy to pick because the beans are more visible. Stringless varieties of pole bean are popular because the pods are usually

more tender, and they stay in good condition longer.

WATER VEGETABLES AS REQUIRED

A dry spell at this time of year can result in a check to the growth of young plants, and watering may be necessary. Leafy vegetables such as cabbage and spinach respond well, giving an increased yield at harvest time if they have received a steady water supply throughout the growing season. All transplanted vegetables should be watered after planting until they are well established. Other vegetables, however, should not be watered too soon because watering stimulates leafy growth that may be at the expense of flowering and crop production. Beans and peas should not normally be watered until they have started to flower (unless the plants are actually wilting), but once flowering begins, regular watering will help the flowers to set and promote the formation of a good supply of tender beans.

plant vegetables in containers

Not everyone has room for a vegetable plot, but almost every garden has sufficient space for a few vegetables in pots and growing bags on the patio. If the right varieties are chosen, the harvest can be surprisingly good. When using pots and tubs, ensure they have sufficient drainage holes and place a layer of crocks or other coarse drainage material at the base before filling with compost.

1 Prepare tubs and large pots in the normal way. Ensure that there are sufficient drainage holes and place a layer of crocks or other coarse drainage material over the base before adding soil mix (below). The mix can be soilless or loam-based, as you prefer.

3 Growing bags can also be used for vegetables other than tomatoes (below). A bush-type zucchini plant (one plant per bag—it will grow quite large) will give a good crop, and try climbing beans in growing bags placed at the base of fences or walls for the plants to climb up. Both crops need frequent watering.

2 Tomatoes, eggplants (below), and sweet bell peppers are among the most commonly grown vegetables in tubs, and young plants that have been hardened off can be planted out now. Add water-retaining granules to the compost to cut down the amount of watering required.

4 Other vegetables that can be tried in tubs or growing bags include potatoes, beets, kohlrabi, carrots, bush beans (below), lettuce, and radish. Choose fast-maturing, compact-growing varieties —there are several which have been bred specifically for growing in containers on patios or balconies.

▼ *Zucchini make excellent subjects for a growing bag, but they will need frequent and careful watering.*

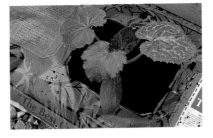

the garden in summer

Summer often appears to be the culmination of the gardeners' year—the season that bears the fruits of efforts to encourage seeds to germinate and plants to grow. Much of its success, however, results from soil preparation that would have been carried out earlier, usually in winter. The days are long, the weather warm and sunny, and what better place to be than in your garden, enjoying the tranquillity and the rewarding harvest of home-grown fruits and vegetables.

early summer

The garden retains the freshness of spring while the floral bounty of summer starts to unfold. While there's still plenty to do, the hectic spring rush is calming down, and we can enjoy the garden at a more leisurely pace, especially as the daylight hours stretch out into the evening now.

The weather and watering

While everyone longs for a good spell of settled, warm sunny weather, we also need enough rain to keep the plants growing strongly, but droughts do seem to be becoming more common every year. Early summer is often a time of mixed weather with heavy storms

depositing gallons of water on the garden within a few minutes, but gardeners need to be prepared to get out the hose or watering can if the weather remains dry for more than a few days. It pays to conserve water by adding organic matter to the soil to increase its water-holding capacity, and by mulching to prevent too much water evaporating from the soil surface.

Plants and produce

At least, though, it's safe to stop worrying about damaging night frosts, and all those tender plants can now go outside, but do take care to harden them off properly first. Conditions should be near perfect for plant growth, and fast-growing plants now need regular care to keep them tied into their supports.

The early spring-flowering shrubs such as forsythia have had their moment of

◀ *Flower borders are bursting with color in early summer. Opposites on the color wheel, yellow and purple provide a striking contrast.*

glory, and once the flowers are over it's time to think about pruning the plants. Roses will soon be in full bloom, but all too often the display is spoiled by pests and diseases. The latter can be prevented by regular fungicide sprays, and plants must be checked regularly for pests and treated with the appropriate controls as soon as any are spotted.

The perfect foil for burgeoning flower borders is an emerald-green lawn. Keep the lawn watered, fed, and regularly mown (not too short) for the best results. And note that the vegetable garden should now be producing an increasing number of crops to harvest; this is the time of year when they really taste their best. Toward the end of the summer the strawberries will be ready for picking, with the promise of raspberries and the rest of the soft fruit crop soon to follow.

EARLY SUMMER TASKS

Ornamental garden

- Plant out tender bedding plants and sow biennials and perennials
- Prune spring-flowering shrubs and trim hedges
- Trim alpines after flowering
- Tie climbers to their supports; increase them by layering
- Tie in border plants and apply a liquid feed; deadhead as appropriate
- Cut down euphorbias that are past their best
- Treat pests as they appear
- Divide and replant flag irises and primulas (primroses) after flowering
- Take cuttings of dianthus (pinks)
- Feed and water plants in containers
- Spray roses against pests and diseases as necessary. Remove suckers
- Lift and divide narcissus (daffodils)
- Mulch borders to keep down weeds

▲ *It's now safe to set even the more tender bedding plants outdoors.*

Lawns

- Continue regular mowing and watering, weeding, and feeding lawns as necessary
- Mow areas of naturalized bulbs
- Deal with moles as molehills appear

Kitchen garden

- Continue weeding and watering as necessary
- Earth up potatoes and lift early varieties
- Sow late crops such as radishes, summer spinach, lettuces, and turnips
- Continue planting out beans, leeks, and winter brassicas
- Pinch out beans and harvest early peas
- Plant out outdoor tomatoes and peppers
- Check vegetables for caterpillars
- Remove runners from strawberries
- Thin young tree fruits
- Summer prune red and white currants, gooseberries

▲ *Sweet bell peppers will grow well outdoors in mild areas.*

Greenhouse

- Damp down and ventilate regularly
- Feed developing food crops (tomatoes, cucumbers, sweet bell peppers, eggplant)
- Remove male flowers from cucumbers and side-shoots from tomatoes
- Control pests such as whitefly and red spider mite
- Sow cinerarias
- Move pot plants such as azaleas and winter cherry outside for the summer

plants in season

The season of plenty is beginning now, with more and more plants coming into flower by the day. Roses are among the top favorites in bloom this month, but there are many other flowering shrubs. Border plants are also looking particularly good.

▼ Papaver 'Patty's Plum': individual poppy flowers tend to be short-lived, but there is usually a long succession of blooms.

▲ *Cranesbills, or perennial geraniums, make soft mounds of attractively cut leaves topped by piercing purple-blue flowers.*

▼ *Elegant spires of flowers make the delphinium a classic border plant, perfect for a "cottage garden" effect.*

PERENNIALS AND BEDDING PLANTS

Achillea filipendulina 'Gold Plate' (yarrow)
Ageratum (floss flower)
Althaea
Aquilegia vulgaris (granny's bonnet)
Astrantia major (Hattie's pincushion)
Campanula (bellflower)
Coreopsis (tickseed)
Delphinium elatum hybrids
Dianthus (carnation, pink)
Dictamnus albas (burning bush)
Digitalis purpurea (common foxglove)
Fuchsia (bedding varieties)
Geranium
Heuchera (coral flower)
Iris
Lobelia erinus
Lupinus (lupin)
Nepeta × *faassenii* (catmint)
Paeonia (peony)
Papaver orientale (oriental poppy)
Pelargonium

BULBS

Allium
Camassia leichtlinii, C. quamash (quamash)
Iris
Lilium (lily)—pictured below

TREES AND SHRUBS

Abelia x grandiflora
Buddleja alternifolia, B. globosa
Ceanothus (Californian lilac)
Cistus purpureus (rock rose)
Deutzia gracilis
Escallonia
Lonicera periclymenum (common honeysuckle)
Philadelphus (mock orange)
Potentilla (cinquefoil)
Pyracantha (firethorn)
Rhododendron
Rosa (rose)
Spiraea douglasii
Syringa (lilac)
Viburnum plicatum (Japanese snowball bush)
Weigela
Wisteria sinensis (Chinese wisteria)

sowing and planting

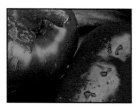

The sowing season for vegetables is not yet over. In fact there are several types that can be sown now to extend the season and provide crops in late summer. It's also time to think even further ahead and plant out some of the vegetables that will see you through the winter days.

Sow successional crops

Although the main sowing season is over, there are several vegetables that can be sown successfully over the next few weeks for picking in late summer or early fall. They include radishes, carrots, beets, corn salad, lettuces, kohlrabi, arugula, radicchio, turnips, rutabaga, and spinach. Care should be taken with the choice of varieties as the summer wears on because some are more suitable for late-season sowing than others, being resistant to bolting, or to diseases such as mildew.

Lettuce often fails to germinate when sown in summer because it is subject to high temperature dormancy. This means lettuce should be sown with extra care during hot spells. Make sure you water the drills well immediately before sowing to reduce the soil temperature, and sow in the cool of evening for the best results.

PLANT OUT WINTER CROPS

Winter crops such as Brussels sprouts, cabbages, kale, and leeks can be planted out now. All brassicas (members of the cabbage family) need to be planted very firmly because loose planting leads to loosely formed heads without a dense heart, and "blown" sprouts. In all but very heavy soils, firm newly planted brassicas very thoroughly with the sole of your boot; firm again after watering. If you gently tug a leaf of the plant, the leaf should tear before the plant's roots move in the soil.

◀ *Fast-maturing radish can be sown at intervals all through the summer to provide a succession of young, tender roots.*

plant bell peppers outdoors

Once the risk of frost is over, tender crops such as sweet bell peppers (capsicums) and tomatoes can be planted safely out of doors. Make sure the young plants are thoroughly hardened off before setting them in their final positions.

1 Sturdy young plants that are filling a 3¼in/8cm pot with roots are the best size for planting out. Select vigorous, healthy plants with deep green leaves; white root tips should be just visible through the drainage holes at the base of the pot.

2 Remove the plant from its pot by placing two fingers either side of the plant's stem, inverting the pot and knocking the rim against a hard surface, e.g., the edge of a table. The whole root-ball should slide out of the pot (left).

3 Dig a hole with a trowel in well-prepared soil in the vegetable garden and set the plant in it (left), covering the top of the root-ball with soil and firming in well with your knuckles. Water well immediately after planting.

4 If the weather should turn cool or windy after planting, young plants can be protected by covering them with a cloche. As the plants grow taller, two cloches can be turned on end to still provide some shelter.

5 Peppers and other tender vegetable crops also grow well when planted in growing bags on a patio (above), often a warmer, more sheltered position. Set two plants per bag for the best results. Cut a cross in the plastic and tuck the flaps under to make the planting hole. Plants in growing bags need regular watering and liquid feeding, particularly in dry or windy weather.

◀ *Green bell peppers are simply fruits picked when immature. If allowed, they will ripen to red, orange, or yellow, according to variety.*

mid-summer

Flowers are at their peak in most gardens now, and deadheading, watering, staking, and harvesting will keep gardeners busy. Make the most of the good weather to enjoy the garden, and on warm nights also make sure you stroll around after dusk to appreciate the night-scented flowers.

Lawns

Lawn grasses are among the first plants to show distress in dry spells. Continue mowing the grass frequently to keep it looking good, but raise the height of the mower blades a little to give the lawn more drought resistance. As long as the clippings are very short, they can be left on the lawn in dry spells to help conserve moisture.

Plants

Rock garden plants and some early-flowering perennials will look better for being tidied up now, so once flowering has finished, cut them back hard. Continue to prune deciduous, flowering shrubs after flowering, too, to keep them to the required size. Many shrubs can also be propagated from semiripe cuttings throughout this month and next.

▶ *Keep the flower borders looking their best by regular deadheading, feeding, and supporting throughout the summer.*

Harvesting

In the kitchen garden there should be plenty to harvest, but successional sowings continue to extend the season. Keep fruiting plants such as beans, marrows, and peas well watered while flowering to insure a good crop. Watering throughout the garden is likely to take up a considerable amount of time in mid-summer. Outdoor plants in windowboxes, hanging baskets, and pots, particularly, can start suffering from water shortage within hours on hot, cloudless summer days.

Pest and diseases

Fungus diseases can be a particular problem in warmer weather, and a routine of preventive fungicide sprays is a good idea for susceptible plants. Pests should be treated as soon as they are seen—preventive spraying is not generally applicable as far as insecticides are concerned.

MID-SUMMER TASKS

General

- Check plants for pests and diseases and treat them early
- Continue watering without wasting water
- Install garden lighting

Ornamental garden

- Prune shrubs that have finished flowering as necessary; prune wisteria
- Continue trimming hedges
- Prick out perennials and biennials sown earlier
- Deadhead flowers and cut back rock plants that are becoming untidy
- Start to take semiripe cuttings of shrubs

- Look out for fall-flowering bulbs and Lilium candidum (Madonna lilies) and plant as early as possible
- Cut back early-flowering border plants to encourage a second flush
- Deadhead, prune, and water plants in containers
- Cut flowers for use indoors

- Stake and tie dahlias; disbud them if large blooms are required
- Check Aster novi-belgii (Michaelmas daisies) for mildew, and treat if necessary
- Order spring bulbs from mail order catalogs

▲ Garden lighting will add atmosphere and enable you to continue to enjoy the garden after dusk.

Lawns

- Leave clippings on the grass occasionally
- Increase mowing height in times of drought

Water garden

- Top up ponds with fresh water as necessary
- Continue to feed fish to help build them up for winter

Kitchen garden

- Harvest vegetables regularly as soon as they are ready
- Check potatoes for potato blight
- Pick herbs for drying, freezing, and use in pot pourri
- Thin seedlings
- Plant cold-stored potatoes for a fall crop

- Continue planting winter vegetables
- Water beans when flowering
- Remove straw on strawberry beds after fruiting, and cut the foliage from strawberries not required for propagation. Root strawberry runners

- Cut off foliage affected by silver leaf on plums and other stone fruit
- Start summer-pruning of trained apples and pears
- Cut down summer-fruiting raspberry canes after fruiting

▲ Sow herbs such as coriander ready for potting up for use over the winter months.

Greenhouse

- Continue training food crops
- Renew shading as necessary; continue watering, ventilating, and damping down

- Use electric fans to circulate cool air
- Prick off cineraria seedlings
- Pot up rooted cuttings
- Sow herbs for winter use

- Avoid blossom end rot on tomatoes by watering regularly to prevent plants flagging. Feed cucumbers, bell peppers, and tomatoes, etc. with high-potash fertilizer and pick fruits regularly as they ripen

plants in season

Annuals are in full flower this month. Easy to grow, they make most effective, colorful garden plants. Summer bedding plants are also in their prime. Trees are looking majestic in full leaf, and there are plenty of flowering shrubs to brighten the garden.

▼ *Lavender not only brings a splash of color to the garden, it also contributes to the marvellous aromas found at this time of year.*

PLANTS WITH SCENTED FLOWERS

Achillea
Alstroemeria (Peruvian lily)
Althaea
Astilbe
Astrantia major
  (Hattie's pincushion)
Begonia semperflorens
Campanula (bellflower)
Chrysanthemum maximum
Coreopsis (tickseed)
Delphinium elatum hybrids
Dianthus (carnation, pink)
Digitalis purpurea
  (common foxglove)
Echinops ritro (globe thistle)
Erigeron (fleabane)
Gaillardia × *grandiflora*
Geranium
Geum (avens)
Gypsophila paniculata
Helenium
Hemerocallis (day lily)
Heuchera (coral flower)
Kniphofia (red hot poker)
Lathyrus (everlasting pea)
Lupinus (lupin)
Nepeta × *faassenii* (catmint)
Nicotiana alata (tobacco plant)
Oenothera (evening primrose)
Pelargonium
Penstemon
Phlox paniculata (perennial phlox)
Romneya coulteri (tree poppy)
Scabiosa caucasica
  (pincushion flower)
Solidago (Aaron's rod)

BULBS

Cardiocrinum giganteum
Crocosmia × *crocosmiiflora*
Eucomis bicolor (pineapple flower)
Gladiolus
Lilium (lily)

TREES AND SHRUBS

Abelia floribunda, *A.* × *grandiflora*
Catalpa bignonioides (Indian bean tree)
Ceanothus (Californian lilac)
Cistus (rock rose)
Clethra alnifolia (sweet pepper bush)
Cytisus battandieri (pineapple bloom)
Escallonia
Eucryphia
Fuchsia magellanica
Genista (broom)
Helianthemum (rock rose)
Hydrangea macrophylla
Hypericum calycinum (Aaron's beard)
Lavandula (lavender)
Lonicera periclymenum (common honeysuckle)
Olearia × *haastii* (daisy bush)
Philadelphus (mock orange)
Rosa (rose)
Vinca major (greater periwinkle), *V. minor*
  (lesser periwinkle)

▲ Lupins are particularly prone to damage by heavy rain if they are not adequately staked. This variety is 'Gallery Pink'.

▼ Free-flowering pelargoniums are a popular choice for hanging baskets and other containers. Deadheading will extend the flowering season.

planting and harvesting

Herbs are valuable in the garden for their appearance and fragrance, and indispensable in the kitchen. While nothing beats the flavor of fresh herbs, there are several easy ways in which they can be preserved. Mid-summer, while they are at their peak, is the time to pick them for storing.

Harvesting herbs

The best time to pick herbs is in the morning of a dry day, waiting until the dew has dried off the foliage. Pick young stems, and do not wash them unless it is absolutely essential.

The age-old method of preservation is drying; it is simple to do and gives good results. Tie the herbs in small, loose bunches—if they are too large, they will go moldy in the center. Hang them upside down in a warm, dry, airy place. The atmosphere in the kitchen is usually too moist and an airing cupboard (with the door ajar), spare bedroom, or garden shed may be more suitable.

For faster results, herbs can be laid on racks in a very cool oven overnight. They can also be dried in batches in a microwave, though it is often difficult to get the timing right with this method.

Once the stems and foliage are completely dry, the herbs can be crumbled and stored in tightly lidded jars for use as required.

▲ *Select fresh, young shoots of herbs for preserving, picking them early in the morning, once the dew has dried off the leaves.*

FREEZING HERBS

Freezing tends to give fresher-tasting results than drying, and is particularly useful for herbs that do not dry well, such as basil.

Pick over the herbs and remove tough stems, then place them (single varieties or a mixture) in an electric blender and almost cover with water. Whizz them in the blender until the herbs are finely chopped, then pour the resulting mixture of herbs and water into ice cube trays and freeze. Add one or two of the ice cubes to soups, sauces or casseroles.

plant out leeks

Leeks are an invaluable winter vegetable, withstanding almost any amount of cold weather. Seedlings from sowings made in trays or a seedbed in spring will now be ready for transplanting to their final positions.

1 Prepare the ground for leeks thoroughly, because they need to be planted deeply in order to develop the maximum length of tender white stems. The crop will benefit from some well-rotted compost or manure worked into the soil before planting.

2 Knock the underside of the seedflat smartly to loosen the roots, and tease the young plants apart carefully. Gather up a handful of seedlings with the bases of the plants in line, and trim the long, straggly roots and leaf tips with a pair of sharp scissors to make the plants easier to handle (right).

3 Make planting holes with a wooden dibble some 6 in/15 cm deep and the same distance apart. A leek seedling is simply dropped into each hole, leaving the holes open (left). Make sure the leek drops right to the base of the hole: that's why it's best to trim back the roots.

4 Once planting is complete, water the plants gently; this washes enough soil over the roots to anchor them in place. Each planting hole is filled with water and then left to drain (right).

5 If the weather is very dry shortly after planting, the seedlings may need to be watered again once or twice, but otherwise they usually need no further attention. They will be ready for harvesting in fall and winter.

◄ *Continue to keep the vegetable garden free of weeds as far as possible. Increasing numbers of crops are approaching maturity now.*

late summer

The garden is at its best now, but despite the profusion of summer flowers and foliage, the first hints of fall soon make themselves felt. Dusk begins to come earlier, and in the mornings there is a hint of mistiness and heavy dew. It's time to start to prepare for the fall and winter ahead.

In dry seasons, watering will be a priority in both the flower and kitchen gardens. Weeds may not be in such profusion as in early summer but must still be dealt with promptly if they are not to get out of hand.

Herbaceous and mixed borders can look splendid this month, but weeding, mulching, staking, and tying-in plants must continue. Staking is particularly important now because late-summer storms can bring heavy rain and strong winds to wreck the display. Some of the border plants that were at their best earlier may now need to be trimmed in order to allow later-flowering subjects to be seen.

Also take steps to control various pests and diseases before they have a chance to inflict too much damage—mildew on plants such as *Aster novi-belgii*

(Michaelmas daisies) is very bad in some years, but can be kept at bay by regular fungicide spraying of susceptible subjects.

In the kitchen garden there is often a glut as all the crops come to fruition at once. Picking must continue regularly because if pods or fruits of crops such as beans, peas, zucchini, and squash are allowed to mature, the plants will stop producing further crops.

Surplus produce should be stored away for the winter and next spring, and now is the time for freezing, canning, and jelly and pickle making.

This is also the time of year when many gardeners take a couple of week's holiday, leaving the garden to fend for itself. This need not mean facing disaster on the return home; a little work put in before the holiday will be more than repaid afterward.

▶ *There should still be plenty of color from the flower borders for some weeks to come. Deadheading prolongs the flowering period.*

LATE SUMMER TASKS

Ornamental garden

- Remove dead flowers from lavender and thyme, and clip plants
- Take cuttings of tender and dubiously hardy perennials to overwinter
- Continue to spray Michaelmas daisies against mildew
- Weed borders and tidy up the plants
- Feed late-flowering border plants

- Check dahlias and chrysanthemums for earwig damage
- Pot up mint for winter use
- Trim back border plants to allow late-flowering varieties to be seen
- Order bare-root shrubs and trees for fall planting
- Plant container-grown shrubs and border plants, keeping them well watered

- Clear out faded window boxes and hanging baskets, and replant them for winter interest; continue to feed and water others
- Trim evergreen hedges for the last time
- Remove annuals that have finished flowering
- Plant Lilium candidum (Madonna lily) bulbs
- Continue to take semiripe cuttings of shrubs

Lawns

- Prepare the site for sowing grass shortly

Water garden

- Aerate ponds in sultry weather

◀ Firm strawberries well when planting, and make sure the soil remains moist.

Kitchen garden

- Make a herb garden and take cuttings of shrubby herbs
- Plant strawberries
- Summer-prune trained fruit
- Pick early apples as they ripen
- Continue to harvest vegetables and soft fruit, freezing or storing gluts for later use

- Feed outdoor tomatoes with high-potash fertilizer; remove yellowed lower leaves
- Blanch leeks by drawing up soil around the stems
- Sow prickly-seeded spinach or spinach beet for a spring crop
- Sow spring cabbages in a seedbed

- Sow Japanese onions
- Thin out new summer-fruiting raspberry canes, tying in the rest to supports
- Pick fall-fruiting raspberries as they ripen
- Provide squash and pumpkins with straw to keep fruits off wet soil
- Ripen onions by bending their necks

▼ Early apples are ready for picking when the fruit separates easily from the spur.

Greenhouse

- Pick melons as they ripen. Continue to pick tomatoes and other food crops
- Regulate watering of food crops carefully
- Watch weather forecasts and close down vents on cooler nights

- Sow cyclamen seed for houseplants; start old cyclamen tubers into growth
- Take cuttings of pelargoniums
- Pot up freesia corms for scented winter flowers

- Check greenhouse heaters are in good working order

plants in season

Herbaceous borders are perhaps at their peak this month, being filled with color and flowers. Hanging baskets, window boxes, and tubs should still be looking good, too, though they may be running out of steam if watering and feeding have not been kept up.

▼ *Among the best of the late-flowering border plants are the aromatic, flat, colorful heads of achillea.*

TREES AND SHRUBS

Buddleja davidii
Campsis radicans (trumpet creeper)
Clerodendrum bungei (glory flower)
Eucryphia
Fuchsia
Hebe
Hibiscus syriacus
Hydrangea macrophylla
Hypericum (St. John's Wort)
Lonicera (honeysuckle)
Rosa (rose)

BULBS

Crocosmia × *crocosmiiflora*
Cyclamen purpurascens
Eucomis bicolor (pineapple flower)
Gladiolus hybrids
Lilium (lily)

▼ *The sweet scent of lilies continues to be a major feature of the garden.*

▲ *Many rose varieties have several flushes of bloom to carry them through the summer and into early fall.*

PERENNIALS

Acanthus (bear's breeches)
Achillea (yarrow)
Aconitum (aconite)
Anemone × *hybrida*
Aster
Begonia semperflorens
Chrysanthemum
Gazania
Helenium
Helianthus annuus (sunflower)
Hemerocallis (day lily)
Kniphofia (red hot poker)
Phlox paniculata (perennial phlox)
Romneya coulteri (tree poppy)
Rudbeckia (coneflower)

sowing and planting

The reward for all your work in the vegetable garden becomes apparent as more and more crops are ready to harvest. It's still time to be thinking ahead, however; there are crops to be sown or planted now for next season, and winter crops to look after for the more immediate future.

Spinach for spring

The tender green leaves of spinach make a very welcome vegetable in the spring, and plants sown now are less likely to run to seed than crops sown in the spring for summer use. Traditionally, prickly-seeded varieties of spinach are the ones to sow in late summer and early fall, using round-seeded types in spring. Many modern hybrids are equally good for both seasons, however.

Sow seeds thinly in drills about 12in/30cm apart; water the soil the day before if conditions are dry. Once the seedlings emerge, thin them to around 9in/23cm. Depending on the weather, there may be leaves to harvest from late fall right through the winter, but the most reliable flush of foliage will be in early spring. Earlier cropping can be obtained if the seedlings are covered with cloches.

JAPANESE ONIONS

Onion varieties such as 'Express Yellow' and 'Senshyu Semi-globe Yellow' are specially bred for sowing in late summer. They are winter hardy, and will give the earliest crop next year in early to mid-summer. The timing of sowing is fairly critical, however. Plants that are sown  too soon often run to seed prematurely in the spring, whereas those which are sown too late either give a disappointing crop of small bulbs or die out over winter. Gardeners in cold districts need to sow one or two weeks ahead of those in milder areas. Sow in rows 9–12in/23–30cm apart, and leave the seedlings until spring; then thin them to 4in/10cm apart. Water the drills before sowing, and damp them down frequently in the days following if the weather is hot, to cool the soil and improve germination.

◄ *Sow plenty of rows of spinach. The leaves shrink so much when they are cooked that you always need more than you think you will.*

plant strawberries

The yield and quality of strawberries usually drops off after three years of cropping, and it is advisable to think about replacing the bed with new plants after this time. Replacing one-third of the plants in the strawberry bed each year means that you will continue to have strawberries to harvest every year.

1 Strawberry plants are prone to a number of virus diseases that reduce their yields, and it is a good idea to buy certified virus-free stock to give them the best possible start.

3 Well-rooted runners in small pots or peat blocks can be bought from garden centers, or by mail order from specialist suppliers. They should be planted as soon as possible after arrival, spacing them around 12–18in/30–45cm apart in rows 3ft/90cm apart (below).

2 Prepare the soil well before obtaining the plants, adding well-rotted organic matter and clearing away all traces of weeds, so difficult to control in any well-established strawberry bed.

4 Plant with a trowel (above), firming the plants in thoroughly with the sole of your boot. The crown of the plant should be just level with the soil surface. Water after planting, using a medium fine spray on the watering can or hose to avoid disturbing the roots (below).

◄ *Crops for harvesting in winter, such as cabbages, should be coming along strongly. Keep them weed free, and water them in dry weather.*

lawns and water gardens

As long as the weather has not been too dry, lawns should still be looking good. Next month is the best time to start a new lawn from seed—prepare the ground for it now. Water gardens should also be in good condition, with plenty of color and interest from both floating plants and marginals.

Keeping ponds healthy

Now that floating plants such as *Nymphaea* (water lilies) have spread their leaves to shade much of the water surface from direct sun, any problems with green water due to algae that occurred earlier in the summer should be over.

Lilies and similar plants should still have plenty of flowers to add color to the water garden scene, but some of the older leaves will be yellowing and starting to die back. Remove these from the water as soon as you notice them; it is important to keep decaying plant refuse out of the pond as far as possible. Also continue to regularly check the undersides of lily leaves for the transparent blobs of snails' eggs, and remove any found. Water snails can be a serious plant pest, and snails or eggs are often introduced unwittingly when new plants are bought. The ramshorn snail is the only satisfactory species for garden pools.

AERATE POND WATER

Normally, the water in a pond takes in oxygen and releases carbon dioxide at the surface, but in sultry, thundery weather this process becomes very slow or may stop altogether.
Fish in the pool can be badly affected, and can sometimes be seen at the surface of the pool gulping in air: if nothing is done they may die. The effect is worst at night, when pond plants are adding to the carbon dioxide content of the water.

 The simple remedy is to stir up the water to increase its surface area and allow some of the carbon dioxide to escape. This can be done by leaving fountains or waterfalls running, by stirring the water vigorously with a stick or aiming a forceful jet from a hose into the pool.

▲ *Waterfalls not only look and sound attractive, they can help to keep the water in a pool well-aerated—often vital in thundery weather.*

▶ *A well-established, well-kept lawn sets off the whole of the rest of the garden. It will soon be time to start making new lawns.*

prepare sites for sowing grass

Early fall is the best time to sow seed for a new lawn, but now is the time to start preparing the soil. Remember that the grass is going to be a permanent feature for years to come, so it is well worth making sure that the basic preparation is thorough. This is your only chance to get soil conditions right.

1 Clear the site of existing turf, cultivated trees, shrubs, plants and weeds. It is especially important to get rid of perennial weeds because they will be very difficult to control once the lawn is established. Use a weedkiller such as glyphosate where necessary.

2 Once the site is cleared of plant growth, remove any other obstructions there may be, such as large stones, paving slabs and so on (right). The cleared site can then be levelled, filling in dips, and flattening out bumps.

3 If the site slopes steeply it may be necessary to reduce the gradient or construct terraces. Where this sort of work is essential, remove the topsoil and stack it nearby, adjusting the levels by moving subsoil. Respread the topsoil evenly once the work is completed.

PREPARING FOR A NEW LAWN

Turf is the quickest way to make a new lawn, giving virtually instant results. Although soil preparation for turf does not need to be quite as painstaking as for seed sowing, it is still worth thoroughly cultivating the area to be turfed well in advance, removing perennial weeds, stones, etc., and adding a long-lasting fertilizer to get the grass off to a good start.

4 Check the structure and condition of the soil. Add well-rotted organic matter such as garden mix to improve heavy and light soils. Give it a final once-over before sowing (left).

the garden in fall

As poets might say, this is the season of mellow fruitfulness; a time when a garden's final fling of flowers and foliage becomes apparent before the darker days and cool weather of late fall and early winter. There's plenty of tidying up to do, but it's also a time to look ahead and to start making preparations for the following year. Seed and plant catalogs can be collected for reading during the short days of winter.

early fall

Many of the early-fall tasks involve clearing away the debris of the summer season, but there's also plenty of sowing and planting to do. Warm, sunny days and an abundance of bright flowers, foliage, and fruits make the melancholy job of tidying up after the summer a much more pleasant affair.

Although fall marks the end of the main growing season, it is still a busy time in the garden. There are crops to be gathered, leaves to sweep up, and tender plants to be protected before the first frost arrives. Misty mornings, heavy dew, and cool weather combine to make ideal conditions for fungus diseases; regular checks and prompt treatment where appropriate are necessary to prevent plant losses.

The dying leaves of deciduous trees and shrubs often make a remarkable display of brilliant color, but all too soon the show is ended by gales which bring the leaves tumbling down. Dead leaves must be removed from garden ponds, lawns, alpine plants, paths, and patios before they can do damage or become a nuisance, and leaf clearing can be a major job in large gardens.

Beds and borders should still be putting on a show with late-blooming plants if varieties have been chosen wisely. Tidy spent border plants and old stems to show off these late-flowering plants to advantage. Weeds continue to thrive and need removing regularly.

Fall is an excellent time for planting both bare-root and container-grown plants. It is also time to plant spring bulbs, always a pleasant task, as we can look forward to their flowers signaling that winter will be over in a few months' time.

There are seeds to be sown in early fall, too. Some hardy annuals will brave the winter cold and produce early flowers next summer if sown outdoors now. In the vegetable garden peas and some beans can be tried, and fall is the perfect time to sow a new lawn.

◄ *Border plants such as the architectural, steely-blue* Eryngium *continue to make a bold display well into the fall months.*

EARLY FALL TASKS

General

- Watch out for fungus diseases around the garden
- Deal with fallen leaves
- Clean and put away garden furniture

Ornamental garden

- Plant spring bulbs
- Sow hardy annuals to overwinter
- Take cuttings of evergreens and plant hardy evergreen shrubs
- Move tender plants under cover before the frosts. Provide outdoor protection for slightly hardier ones

- Replace annuals and summer bedding with spring bedding as they fade
- Continue to clear containers and replant with bulbs and spring bedding
- Clear and weed around fall-flowering bulbs and perennials

- Prepare sites for fall planting of bare-root trees and shrubs
- Protect decorative berries from birds
- Take cuttings of old-fashioned and shrub roses
- Check ties and stakes on trees, and adjust if necessary

▲ *Daffodil bulbs should be planted as soon as they become available in the shops.*

Lawns

- Sow new lawns
- Rake and aerate lawns, and give them a fall feed
- Repair bald patches, broken edges, bumps, and dips

- Deal with toadstools
- Water garden
- Net ponds against falling leaves

- Remove tender pond plants before the frosts

Kitchen garden

- Plant spring cabbage
- Harvest maincrop potatoes
- Support winter brassicas if necessary
- Lift maincrop carrots and beets
- Thin out seedlings

- Pick outdoor tomatoes and clear away plants
- Harvest pumpkins and squashes before the first frosts
- Sow winter lettuce under a cloche or tunnel

- Plant onion sets for an early crop
- Continue picking apples and pears

▼ *Prick off cyclamen seedlings as soon as they are large enough to handle.*

Greenhouse

- Ventilate the greenhouse and water plants with care
- Bring pot plants such as azaleas and solanums back indoors
- Pick remaining food crops (such as bell peppers and tomatoes) and discard the plants

- Clean the framework and glass where appropriate
- Plant bulbs in pots and bowls for forcing
- Pot up cineraria and cyclamen seedlings
- Continue to take cuttings of tender outdoor plants as an insurance against winter losses

plants in season

Early fall may mark the beginning of the end of the growing season, but it is still filled with color and interest. Late-flowering perennials and bulbs, bright fruit and berries abound; and, depending on the weather conditions, the first of the fiery fall leaf tints from deciduous trees and shrubs make themselves evident.

▲ Perovskia atriplicifolia *'Blue Spire' has attractive, aromatic, gray-green foliage as well as panicles of strikingly blue flowers.*

▶ *The butterfly's favorite, Sedum spectabile. The variety 'Iceberg' has pure white flowers instead of the more familiar pink.*

▼ *The dainty flowers of Cyclamen hederifolium are held above attractively marbled leaves that persist right through the winter.*

TREES AND SHRUBS

Caryopteris × *clandonensis*
Ceanothus (Californian lilac)
Clerodendrum bungei (glory flower),
    C. trichotomum
Erica (heath)
Hebe
Hydrangea macrophylla
Leycesteria formosa
    (Himalayan honeysuckle)
Malus (crab apple)
Perovskia atriplicifolia
Rosa (flowers and hips) (rose)
Vinca major (greater periwinkle),
    V. minor (lesser periwinkle)

PERENNIALS AND BEDDING PLANTS

Achillea (yarrow)
Aconitum napellus (aconite)
Anemone × *hybrida*
Aster
Eryngium (sea holly)
Helenium
Hemerocallis (day lily)
Kniphofia (red hot poker)
Rudbeckia (coneflower)
Schizostylis coccinea (kaffir lily)
Sedum spectabile (ice plant)
Solidago (Aaron's rod)

BULBS

Amaryllis belladonna
Colchicum (fall crocus)
Crinum × *powellii*
Crocosmia crocosmiiflora
Crocus (fall-flowering species)
Cyclamen
Nerine bowdenii

◀ *The daisy-like flowers of helenium brighten fall borders with their gloriously rich shades of red, bronze, and yellow.*

planting and sowing

As well as harvesting the abundance of crops in the kitchen garden now, keep some continuity of cropping going with further plantings and sowings. A little extra protection from the weather can be gained by sowing under cover. Seedlings from earlier sowings need thinning out or transplanting.

Plant onion sets

Onion sets planted in the fall will give an early crop next year, several weeks before maincrop varieties are ready for harvest. Varieties available for fall planting have been chosen for their hardiness and disease resistance, and include 'Early Yellow Globe,' 'Yellow Spanish,' 'Snow White hybrid,' and the red-fleshed 'Red Hamburger.' Prepare the soil thoroughly and mix in some coarse sand or grit to lighten it if necessary, as fall-planted sets need free-draining conditions. Plant the sets in rows 14in/35cm apart, spacing the sets 4–6in/10–15cm apart in the row. Always plant onion sets with a trowel, because simply pushing the sets into the soil can compact the ground immediately beneath them, making it difficult for the roots to penetrate. Fall-planted onions can be ready to harvest as early as late spring, but they can be stored for only a few weeks.

THIN OUT SEEDLINGS

Seedlings from late sown crops, including lettuce, radish, spinach, and turnips, among others, should be thinned out as soon as they are large enough. This thinning is best carried out in progressive stages to allow for plant losses—thin to half the final recommended spacing first, then remove every other plant later on, as necessary.

Where seedlings are very crowded, great care is necessary to avoid disturbing the roots of the plants which are to remain after thinning. If the weather is dry, water the row of seedlings before thinning to make it easier to tease away the unwanted plants.

◀ *Fall-planted onion sets should produce a crop that is ready for harvesting very early the following summer.*

lettuce for winter

It's great to have been able to cut fresh salads straight from the garden through the summer, and it's something that will be sadly missed over the next few months. However, it is possible to have a supply of winter lettuce from the greenhouse—the plants won't be as succulent and full hearted as summer varieties, but they're still worth growing. Sow the seed now; once the seedlings are large enough, they can be transplanted into growing bags, or direct into the greenhouse border.

1 It's important to choose the right variety of lettuce for growing in the greenhouse in winter because only a few are suitable. It would be wise to check with your local garden center to see what is the best choice.

2 An unheated greenhouse is quite suitable for growing winter lettuce, although heated greenhouses will give a faster-maturing crop. Cold frames and polytunnels can also be used successfully for growing winter salads.

3 Sow the seed thinly on a prepared flat of moist soil mix and cover lightly. Lettuce seed becomes dormant in very hot conditions, so it is important to keep the flat in a well-ventilated, lightly shaded position after sowing.

4 Once the seedlings are showing through, move the flat to full light. Water very carefully to avoid fungus disease. Prick out the seedlings to wider spacings as soon as they are large enough to be handled easily.

▲ *Transplant cabbages to their cropping positions. If preferred, space the young plants closely to obtain "greens" rather than densely hearted cabbages.*

mid-fall

The tidy-up continues as more and more fall leaves hit the ground and late season flowers fade. As the weather becomes increasingly cold, it's time to protect the more delicate plants. Remain on the alert for frosts, though with luck you may find yourself enjoying a warm and sunny Indian summer.

Tidying up

This is often the time when fall leaf color is at its glorious best, but it won't be long before a windy spell brings the leaves to the ground in drifts. Fallen leaves are not so bad when they are dry and crisp, but once rain turns them to a slimy brown sludge they pose a danger

to both plants and people. Regularly remove them from lawns and small, vulnerable plants like alpines before the leaves smother them; also clear them from paths and steps before somebody slips in the decomposing mush and injures themselves.

Cut down spent flowers and dying foliage in herbaceous borders, but don't be too enthusiastic. Some dead, brown stems and leaves have an architectural value, and some seed heads can be particularly decorative.

Cold snap

At what time the first frost arrives, and just how bad the weather might be, depends largely on your particular location. Some regions can rely on mild falls and winters, while others can guarantee that freezing conditions will arrive in the near future. Only

◄ *The deep pink flowers of* Nerine bowdenii *stand out in the fall sunshine. The bulb's foliage does not appear until spring.*

experience can tell you what to expect, but always be prepared for the worst. Better to prepare your dubiously hardy plants for icy weather that does not arrive, than leave them to be killed by a single unexpected cold snap.

Future plans

As more plants in the kitchen garden finish cropping and are removed, vacant soil begins to appear, ready to be dug over for next spring. The earlier winter digging can start the better, allowing you maximum time to complete a task which can be backbreaking if rushed. If the fall weather is too depressing, cheer yourself up by continuing to plant spring-flowering bulbs and spring bedding to give you something to look forward to at the end of the winter, and start thumbing through new seed catalogs to plan next year's sowing program.

MID-FALL TASKS

General

∷ Remove fallen leaves from paths, patios, steps, and lawns and turn them into leaf mold
∷ Clear away all garden debris to avoid pests and diseases
∷ Protect vulnerable plants from rain and cold; beware of early frosts

Ornamental garden

∷ Tidy herbaceous borders and divide border plants; apply bonemeal to borders and around shrubs and trees
∷ Plant tulips and hyacinths; plant lily bulbs as they become available

∷ Remove and burn diseased leaves fallen from roses
∷ Plant bare-root trees and shrubs
∷ Lift and store dahlia roots when the leaves have been blackened by frost

∷ Lift and store gladioli and tuberous begonias
∷ Finish planting spring bedding
∷ Protect newly planted shrubs from strong winds

▲ *This is the ideal time to plant tulips. If planted too early, they start into premature growth.*

Lawns

∷ Lay turf for new lawns
∷ Continue to sweep up leaves and repair damaged areas of grass. Mow as necessary, raising the cutting height of the mower from its summer setting
∷ Apply bulky top-dressing

▼ *Turf establishes quickly in fall conditions, providing a virtually instant new lawn.*

Water garden

∷ Remove submersible pumps from ponds; clean and store them under cover
∷ Tidy pond plants and marginals, removing dead leaves from the water

Kitchen garden

∷ Continue harvesting crops, and store fruit and vegetables. Pick remaining apples and pears. Check fruit and vegetables already in store
∷ Remove vegetable plants as they finish cropping; begin digging and adding organic matter to soil. Start a new vegetable plot if required

∷ Finish planting spring cabbages
∷ Start to fill in seed orders for next year when the catalogs arrive
∷ Take hardwood cuttings of soft fruit
∷ Plant new rhubarb crowns
∷ Prune blackcurrants, blackberries, and hybrid berries

Greenhouse

∷ Remove shading and clean the glass if this has not already been done
∷ Sow Lathyrus odoratus (sweet peas) for early flowers outdoors next year

∷ Take care not to overwater, or splash water about. Remove dead and dying foliage, flowers, and fruit promptly

∷ Ventilate whenever possible to maintain an airy atmosphere
∷ Heat the greenhouse as necessary to maintain a suitable temperature for the plants

plants in season

In most areas, fall color is now at its peak, but it will not be long before the leaves fall. Seed heads and fruit have an ever-increasing role to play in providing interest, but late-flowering perennials and bulbs are still providing color in many gardens.

▼ *The vigorous climber* Parthenocissus quinquefolia, *commonly known as Virginia creeper, has outstanding fall foliage.*

▲ Schizostylis coccinea, *the kaffir lily, is one of the latest-flowering border plants. The variety 'Sunrise' has delicate shell-pink flowers.*

▶ *Purple-leaved* Rosa glauca, *usually grown for its foliage, has the bonus of bunches of glossy red rose hips through the fall.*

TREES AND SHRUBS

Acer (maple)
Berberis (deciduous) (barberry)
Cercidiphyllum japonicum
    (katsura tree)
Cotoneaster
Erica (heath)
Euonymus alatus (burning bush),
    E. europaeus and others
Fothergilla major
Hamamelis
Hippophae rhamnoides (sea buckthorn)
Hydrangea quercifolia
Malus (apple, crab apple)
Parthenocissus (Virginia creeper,
    Boston ivy)
Gaultheria mucronata
Pyracantha (firethorn)
Rosa (hips) (rose)
Skimmia
Sorbus
Vitis coignetiae, V. vinifera
    (grape vine)

PERENNIALS

Aconitum napellus (monkshood)
Anemone × *hybrida*
Aster
Gentiana sino-ornata
Liriope muscari (lily turf)
Physalis alkekengi var. *franchettii* (Chinese
    lantern)
Sedum spectabile (ice plant)

BULBS

Amaryllis belladonna
Colchicum (common crocus)
Crinum × *powellii*
Cyclamen
Galanthus reginae-olgae (snowdrop)
Nerine bowdenii
Schizostylis coccinea (kaffir lily)

harvesting and digging

Most varieties of apples ripening now are suitable for storing for a few weeks but some will keep until next spring, given the right conditions. In the vegetable garden digging continues as crops are cleared from the ground. If you do not yet have a vegetable plot, this is a good time to get started.

Harvest apples and pears

A few apple and pear varieties may need to be left on the tree until late fall, but the majority will have been picked before this.

CLEAR VEGETABLE CROPS

By now, crops such as runner and French beans, summer cabbages, marrows and so on will be more or less finished, and the plants can be cleared away. Unless the spent crop plants are badly diseased, add them to the compost heap to rot down. Tough, woody stems, like those of some brassicas, are very slow to rot and can either be shredded before being added to the heap, or be burned instead. As rows of crop plants are removed, dig the soil over and add compost or manure as available.

▶ *Apples are ripe and ready for picking once the stalk separates easily from the spur when the fruit is lifted gently.*

A number of apple varieties store well, in some instances remaining in good condition until late spring. 'Arkansas Black,' 'Golden Delicious,' 'Gold Rush,' and 'McIntosh' are among the good keepers. Choose unblemished specimens, wrap them individually in sheets of wax paper, and store in a single layer in boxes in a cool garage, cellar, or shed. An alternative method is to place six apples in a strong plastic bag, punch a few holes in the bag with a pencil and tie the top loosely, leaving a small gap. This method is good for varieties that tend to shrivel.

Pears do not store for very long though, and need inspecting daily because they must be eaten immediately they are ripe—they spoil within a day or two.

▶ Wrapping apples separately before storing will help to prevent rot spreading if one of them starts to decay. Only unblemished fruits should be stored; damaged apples will not keep.

start a new vegetable plot

Home-grown vegetables are always welcome, and are very rewarding to grow. While a few vegetables can always be grown in containers on the patio or among the flowers, a dedicated vegetable plot will give you a lot more scope for trying out new, exciting varieties. Make the plot as large as is practical for you to look after.

1 If the vegetable plot is to be made in the lawn, it will be necessary to strip off the turf. This can be done by cutting parallel strips in the grass with a half-moon edging iron, and undercutting the turf with a sharp spade (left). Hiring a turf cutter is worthwhile for large areas.

2 If the turf that has been removed is good quality, it can be relaid elsewhere, or perhaps sold. Otherwise, it can be stacked upside down to rot, when it will make an excellent loam for potting or for mixing with growing soil mixes.

3 The newly-exposed soil should be well cultivated, either digging it by hand (left) or using a mechanical cultivator. Although the cultivator is quicker and easier, double digging (see page 79) allows deeper cultivation and gives better results in the long run—as long as you have the necessary time and stamina to do it. Spread the job over several weeks if necessary.

4 While digging, incorporate as much rotted garden compost or manure into the soil as possible; this improves fertility and soil structure, allowing heavy soils to drain more freely and light soils to become more moisture retentive. The plot should be left roughly dug over winter to allow frost to break down the clods into finer crumbs.

5 A soil testing kit is a worthwhile investment, giving you an idea of the acidity and nutrient levels in the soil (above). Acidity (pH) testing is usually quite accurate and will indicate whether an application of lime is necessary. Nutrient analysis is rather less reliable, but will still give a guide to your soil's fertility.

late fall

Tidying up and preparing plants for the colder weather ahead continues, but planning for next season starts in earnest now, with new plantings to be made and seed orders to be filled out. This is also a good time to have the lawn mower overhauled so that it is ready for next spring.

At this time of year we really notice how the days are shortening. For many gardeners, the only time the garden can be seen in daylight is at weekends, and all the tasks that need to be done have to be crammed into two short days, provided the weather allows.

Fortunately there are few really pressing jobs, but there are still a number of things to be done before the winter months. Firstly, it's important that you protect the more tender plants before the coldest weather arrives. Night frosts will already have struck in many gardens, but the most damaging, sustained freezing temperatures are usually a feature of the winter. Don't forget to insulate outdoor faucets and water pipes, too.

Any damage to plants and garden structures caused by fall gales should be repaired quickly. Fences are particularly prone to problems, so check that fence posts and panels are sound. Garden sheds may also be showing signs of wear and tear. Secure roofing felt that has been loosened, and check for leaks inside, carrying out repairs as necessary. It is vital to have dry storage conditions available for many items including tools and machinery, fertilizers and chemicals, as well as produce such as tree fruit and root vegetables.

Weeds seem to keep growing whatever the weather, and weeding should be carried out as necessary. Since many chemical herbicides need weeds to make rapid growth to work most efficiently, hand weeding is generally the best approach in late fall and winter.

◄ *Make the most of late flowers like sedums. A drab time of year is approaching, with fall color finally extinguished by wind and rain.*

LATE FALL TASKS

General
- Note gaps in the borders and make plans to fill them
- Protect outdoor faucets and water pipes from freezing
- Check bonfire piles for hibernating animals before lighting

Ornamental garden
- Continue tidying borders. Leave top-growth for winter protection in cold areas. In exposed gardens, prune roses lightly to prevent root rock
- Continue planting bare-root trees and shrubs
- Take hardwood cuttings from shrubs
- Protect alpines from rain
- Lift chrysanthemums and box roots to provide cuttings in spring
- Finish planting tulips and hyacinths
- Continue to remove weeds
- Tidy alpines and rock gardens

▼ Floating a ball on the water surface can help to delay the pond freezing.

Lawns
- Give a last cut if necessary, then send mower for service and blade sharpening
- Aerate compacted areas
- Continue turfing in mild spells

Water garden
- Protect ponds and fish from cold. Stop feeding fish

Kitchen garden
- Sow beans and hardy peas for overwintering
- Continue digging spare ground
- Begin harvesting parsnips and Brussels sprouts. Lift some root crops for use in case the soil becomes frozen
- Check summer-planted, cold-stored potatoes and lift when ready. Order new seed potatoes from catalogs for the best choice of varieties
- Plant new fruit trees and bushes; begin winter pruning of fruit
- Continue weeding as necessary
- Protect winter brassicas from birds

Greenhouse
- Ventilate and water with care; use fungicides where necessary
- Bring bulbs for forcing into the light as they develop. Check that plunged bulbs remain moist
- Insulate greenhouses and frames with bubble wrap
- Pinch out the tips of fall-sown Lathyrus odoratus (sweet pea) seedlings at about 4–6in/10–15cm
- Plant Narcissus 'Paper White'
- Sow sprouting seeds for salads

▲ Late fall is an excellent time to plant new fruit trees.

plants in season

As flowers and fall foliage fade, evergreens assume an increasingly important role in bringing interest to the garden. Fruits and berries continue to provide color, and there are still flowers on show as long as the right species have been planted.

▶ *The deep blues of* Gentiana sino-ornata *enrich the garden's color scheme.*

▼ *Viburnum tinus 'Eve Price' offers a frothy interest to the fall garden.*

PERENNIALS

Aster
Helianthus (sunflower)
Gentiana sino-ornata
Iris unguicularis
Liriope muscari (lily turf)

BULBS

Colchicum (fall crocus)
Crocus (fall-flowering species)
Cyclamen
Galanthus reginae-olgae (snowdrop)
Nerine bowdenii
Schizostylis coccinea (kaffir lily)
Sternbergia lutea (fall daffodil)

▼ *Sunflowers provide bold, bright splashes of color and dramatic interest.*

TREES AND SHRUBS

Aucuba japonica (spotted laurel)
Berberis (barberry)
Callicarpa (beauty berry)
Clematis orientale, C. tangutica
Cornus alba (red-barked dogwood)
Cotoneaster
Fatsia japonica (Japanese aralia)
Gaultheria mucronata
Jasminum nudiflorum (jasmine)
Leycesteria formosa (Himalayan
    honeysuckle)
Malus (apple, crab apple)
Prunus × *subhirtella* 'Autumnalis' (fall cherry)
Pyracantha (firethorn)
Rosa (hips) (rose)
Salix alba var. *vitellina* 'Britzensis'
    (white willow)
Skimmia
Sorbus
Symphoricarpos (snowberry)
Vaccinium (bilberry)
Viburnum

planting and sowing

Out-of-season new potatoes may be available from specially-treated seed potatoes planted in the summer; remember to order potatoes from the catalogs for more conventional planting in spring. Unlikely as it seems, it is also time for sowing some vegetables outdoors for next year.

Sowing beans and peas

As long as you sow the right varieties, both beans and peas will overwinter as seedlings to give early crops next year—you could be picking beans and peas by late spring.

Choose a reasonably sheltered site for sowing, on free-draining soil. On heavy soils there is a risk of the seeds rotting, and in this case it is better to sow them in pots or boxes in an unheated greenhouse for planting out in the spring. The crop will not be so early, but it will be more reliable.

Sow beans 4–6in/10–15cm apart in rows 12in/30cm apart; peas are sown rather more closely in the row, at 2–3in/5–7.5cm apart. Depending on your climate zone and prevailing local conditions, your local garden center should be able to advise on the most appropriate varieties to sow in your garden or greenhouse.

▲ *Certain varieties of beans can be sown at this time of year to give a crop late the following spring.*

SUMMER–PLANTED POTATOES

Specially prepared, cold-stored seed potatoes that were planted in the summer produce a crop some two or three months after planting. Check them now, by scraping away some soil to expose the developing tubers. As long as most are large enough to eat they can be lifted when you want to use them. If the weather is mild, the tubers may continue to swell, but most will have finished developing by now. Do not lift the entire crop as you would for maincrop potatoes; they keep best if left in the soil up to mid-winter, insulated from freezing weather with a mulch of straw or dry bracken.

▶ Cherry trees grow particularly well if they are trained against a reasonably sheltered wall or fence. Morello types are most popular.

plant fruit trees and bushes

With the development of dwarfing rootstocks, it is possible for fruit trees such as apples and pears to be grown even in small gardens. Soft fruit bushes such as currants and gooseberries are also easy to grow and provide very welcome crops in the summer.

1 Choose from the wide variety of fruit trees available from specialist nurseries. The plants are often supplied bare-root, by mail order, and should be planted as soon as possible after delivery. Most garden centers stock a reduced but reasonable selection, usually container-grown.

2 Dig out a planting hole wide enough to take the roots of the tree without cramping, and deep enough for the tree to be planted at the same depth it was growing in the nursery. Fork over the base of the hole and add some well-rotted garden compost or planting mixture.

3 Hammer the stake in position before planting the tree to avoid damaging the tree roots. A short stake is all that is necessary. Check that the size of the hole is correct for the tree, then spread the tree roots out in the base of the planting hole (above).

4 Return the excavated soil to the hole, gently jiggling the tree up and down while you do so in order to insure that the soil sifts between the roots. Then you should tread the soil firmly down with the heel of your foot as you proceed (above).

5 When the hole is refilled, attach the tree to the stake with an adjustable tree tie (above). Plant fruit bushes in the same way. If container-grown, remove the root-ball carefully having watered it well a few hours before, put it in the base of the hole and firm the soil around it.

lawns and water gardens

Lawns now start to show signs of wear on heavily used routes as the soil becomes compacted in wet weather. The grass may need a final cut before the mower is sent away for servicing, ready for next spring. Garden ponds should need little attention unless the weather turns particularly cold.

Aerating turf

When the soil is moist it is easily compacted. A frequently trodden route across the lawn will soon become muddy now, with its covering of grass gradually thinning and being worn away.

Since it is important that air can reach the roots of the grass and that surface water can drain away at all times of the year, action should be taken as soon as worn patches are noticed. If the damage is not corrected, moss is likely to develop in place of the grass and will soon spread and take over.

Try to redirect foot traffic away from the worn places if possible. Use a garden fork to spike the compacted areas, driving the prongs into the turf some 3–4in/7.5–10cm deep. Waggle the fork backward and forward gently to enlarge the holes slightly before removing it. Repeat this process over the whole area to leave the rows of holes evenly spaced in both directions.

▲ *Aerating compacted areas of lawn is important to help surface water drain away. It is easily achieved with a garden fork.*

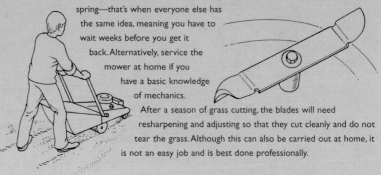

LAWN MOWERS

If the grass has continued to grow, give it a final cut with the blades set high before sending the lawn mower away for its annual service. It is far better to get this done now than wait until next spring—that's when everyone else has the same idea, meaning you have to wait weeks before you get it back. Alternatively, service the mower at home if you have a basic knowledge of mechanics.

After a season of grass cutting, the blades will need resharpening and adjusting so that they cut cleanly and do not tear the grass. Although this can also be carried out at home, it is not an easy job and is best done professionally.

protect ponds from cold weather

If a garden pond freezes over for more than a couple of days, fish may be killed by the toxic gases trapped beneath the ice. The easiest way to prevent this is to install a pond heater.

STOP FEEDING FISH

As the water temperature drops, fish become inactive and will not take food until the water warms up again in the spring. They live off stored body fat through the winter, so it is important to build them up in the early fall. Any food given from now on will sink to the bottom of the pool and rot, polluting the water.

1 At this time of year it is very important to keep the water free of any kind of decaying vegetation, whether this is dead leaves from water plants or fallen leaves from nearby trees. Remove dead and dying leaves regularly, and cover the pool with a net if necessary.

3 If it is not possible to use a pond heater, a ball or hollow polystyrene material floating on the surface of the water will delay freezing as it moves about in the wind (above). And if the water does freeze, boiling water poured around the edge of the ball or polystyrene enables it to be removed leaving a hole in the ice.

2 Remove the pond pump if one is installed, and clean and service it before storing it for the winter (left). If the pool is within reach of a power supply, install a pond heater. This keeps only a small area of the pond free of ice, but allows the air in and toxic gases to escape.

4 Most sunken garden ponds are in no danger of freezing solid, but miniature ponds in half barrels are a different matter—they lack the insulation of the soil around them. In all but mild areas, fish from barrels should be moved under cover. Insulating the barrels with several layers of bubble wrap helps protect water plants.

the garden in winter

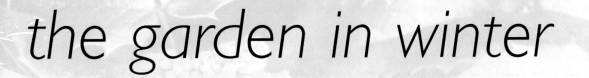

Despite the chilly weather and short hours of daylight, a garden can be a fascinating place during winter. Indeed, many painters have been inspired by frosty mists that encapsulate gardens and plants with a near-mystical aura, creating a wonderland of solitude and reflection. Many shrubs and small bulbous plants are in flower, while evergreen foliage and bright berries never fail to capture attention. The distinctive shapes of many conifers are enhanced when surrounded by a carpet of snow.

early winter

The weather is often entirely unpredictable now. Penetrating frosts and icy winds; continuous dull, depressing rain; or mild, calm, sunny days more like early fall: anything is possible. It may not be the best time of year to be working outside, but seize your opportunities when they arise.

A greenhouse is a real boon for a keen gardener now—whatever the weather, you can get on with growing plants in comparative comfort. In contrast to the often bleak scene outdoors, the greenhouse can be full of color from bulbs and pot plants, and given there's enough heat, you can even begin to start growing certain seeds.

Although the grass has stopped growing and the mower has been put away for the winter, that doesn't mean you can entirely ignore the lawn. This is the time of year when it is most likely to suffer wear and tear, so be prepared to act promptly in order to prevent damage from occurring. Try to avoid walking on it when it is wet and muddy.

Wild birds can be a nuisance at times, but most gardeners appreciate the life they bring to the garden in winter, and are happy to encourage them. The fall season with its fruit, seeds, berries, and insects is over, and it's time to start putting out food on the bird table. But once you start feeding, you must keep it up because the birds will come to rely on you. Remember to provide water for drinking and bathing, too, particularly in freezing weather.

If the garden is looking dull, cheer it up by planting some containers of hardy winter plants like flowering Viola (pansies) and heathers, and variegated foliage plants. In the kitchen garden there will probably still be winter digging and fruit tree pruning to get on with, and don't forget to send off those seed orders before the spring rush.

◀ *Variegated evergreens like* Hedera colchica *'Sulphur Heart' are particularly valuable for brightening the garden in the winter months.*

EARLY WINTER TASKS

General

- Continue winter digging
- Make paths to avoid wear on lawns
- Cover compost heaps to keep out rain

Ornamental garden

- Continue to plant containers for winter and spring interest
- Firm newly planted trees and shrubs after frosts
- Protect the blooms of Helleborus niger (Christmas rose) with straw on the ground
- Check trees and shrubs for root rock or lifting after frosts, refirming them if necessary
- Order flower seeds from catalogs, especially those needing an early start
- Protect young trees against rabbits with tree guards

Lawns

- Avoid walking over frosted grass. Turfing is still possible in mild spells

▲ Make a firm path on well-used routes across lawns to avoid regular treading wearing the grass.

Water garden

- Thaw holes in frozen ponds

Kitchen garden

- Protect fall-sown bean and pea seedlings
- Order seeds from catalogs
- Prune fruit trees

▼ Bulbs of Narcissus 'Paper White' planted now should be in flower in about six weeks.

Greenhouse

- Check the temperature regularly with a maximum/minimum thermometer
- Bring forced bulbs indoors as the flower buds show color
- Sow seeds such as onions and pelargoniums in a heated propagator
- Clean pots and seedtrays ready for the bulk of spring sowing
- Remove faded flowers on cyclamen
- Move cyclamen, Primula (primroses), etc., from the home to the greenhouse when they finish flowering. Spray Indian azaleas with plain water regularly
- Plant more Narcissus 'Paper White' (daffodils) for a succession of flowers

plants in season

This is the time of year when the bark and branches of both trees and shrubs begin to be appreciated; there are some beautiful and striking shapes, textures, and colors to admire. Plenty of leaves, flowers, such as the beautiful snowdrops, and berries, found in seasonal favorites holly and ivy, can be enjoyed too.

▲ *Snowdrops are among the earliest flowers of the year. The double flowers of* Galanthus nivalis *'Flore Pleno' are especially attractive.*

▶ Hamamelis intermedia *'Westerstede'* (witch hazel) bears its fragrant, ragged-petalled flowers on leafless branches.

▼ The sweet-scented, pale yellow flowers of Mahonia japonica *are carried all through the winter, undeterred by the coldest weather.*

TREES AND SHRUBS

Acer, especially *A. capillipes, A. davidii,*
    A. griseum (maple)
Arbutus unedo (strawberry tree)
Aucuba japonica 'Crotonifolia' and others
    (spotted laurel)
Betula, especially *B. ermanii, B. nigra*
    (black birch), *B. papyrifera* (paper birch),
    B. utilis var. *jacquemontii* (Himalayan Birch)
Chimonanthus praecox (wintersweet)
Cornus alba (red-barked dogwood)
Corylus avellana 'Contorta'
    (Harry Lauder's walking stick)
Cotoneaster
Elaeagnus × *ebbingei*
Erica carnea (alpine heath)
Euonymus fortunei, E. japonicus (variegated)
Fraxinus excelsior 'Jaspidea' (European ash)
Hamamelis mollis (Chinese witch hazel)
Hedera (ivy)
Ilex (berry-bearing and variegated
    varieties) (holly)
Jasminum nudiflorum (jasmine)
Lonicera fragrantissima, L. standishii
    (winter honeysuckle)
Mahonia
Prunus serrula, P. × *subhirtella* 'Autumnalis'
    (fall cherry)
Pyracantha (firethorn)
Salix alba, S. babylonica var. *pekinensis*
    'Tortuosa' (dragon-claw willow)
Skimmia japonica
Sorbus
Tilia platyphylos 'Rubra' (red-twigged lime)
Viburnum

PERENNIALS

Helleborus niger (Christmas rose)
Iris unguicularis
Schizostylis coccinea (kaffir lily)

BULBS

Crocus imperati
Cyclamen coum
Galanthus (snowdrop)

pruning and digging

Continue pruning fruit trees during the dormant season, except when the weather is frosty. Winter digging of the vegetable plot should also be proceeding; it is worth digging the ground as deeply as you can, adding plenty of organic matter to improve the soil.

▲ *Protect fall-sown beans and pea seedlings from the worst of the cold weather and wind with mini-polytunnels.*

Protecting beans and peas

Pea and bean seeds sown in the vegetable plot earlier in the fall should have germinated and be showing through the soil by now. Although they are hardy, very cold and windy weather will take its toll of the young plants, so it is worth giving them a little extra protection to see them through the worst spells.

Plants can be protected by glass barn cloches placed over the rows that will keep off the worst of the cold weather and wind, and protect the plants from excess rain. The glass acts as a mini-greenhouse, trapping the warmth of any sun there may be.

Unfortunately glass cloches are very prone to breakage, and can be dangerous, especially where there are children or pets in the garden. Mini-polytunnels are a safer option, although condensation can be a problem, causing fungal rots to affect the seedlings. One of the easiest materials to use is lightweight horticultural blanket that is draped loosely over the crop. Ensure the edges are pegged down or secured to prevent the blanket from blowing away in windy weather.

PRUNING LARGE TREES

Most modern fruit trees are grown on dwarfing or semidwarfing rootstocks, but older trees can grow very tall and wide-spreading, making pruning difficult. If you use a ladder it must be secure; have someone hold it steady. Long-arm pruners make reaching high branches easier; make sure the blades are sharp and the cutting mechanism works smoothly.

PRUNING FRUIT TREES

Pruning in the dormant season stimulates strong, vigorous growth the following spring, and that is why the major pruning of trees trained as restricted forms takes place in summer. Hard winter pruning of apples and pears grown as cordons or espaliers would result in uncontrolled growth. Winter pruning on trained trees should mainly be restricted to removing dead, dying, and diseased wood, and thinning out overcrowded spurs.

Plums should not be pruned in the winter because this invites an invasion by silver leaf disease spores. The disease slowly weakens the trees, and forms bracket fungi on affected branches that release spores mainly during the late fall and winter. The spores enter new wood through fresh wounds. Plums should be pruned in the spring and summer when spores are less likely to be around, and in any case the trees more quickly produce natural resins to seal over pruning cuts. The popular plum variety 'Victoria' is particularly prone to this disease, which also affects almonds, apricots, and cherries, although not usually producing such serious effects as it does on plums.

start winter digging

Since digging is satisfying but hard physical work, large plots should be completed in stages to avoid the back problems that trouble so many over-enthusiastic gardeners. Digging is best carried out as early in the winter as possible, leaving the ground rough for the maximum time to allow frosts to break up the clods of soil.

1 Dig a trench one spit (the depth of the spade's blade) deep across the top of the plot (left). Throw the soil into a wheelbarrow so that it can be moved to the other end of the plot. Try to keep your spine straight while digging.

2 Fork over or chop the soil at the base of the trench with the spade. Move backward and dig a second trench behind the first (left, below). Throw the soil from this to fill the trench in front. Try to turn the soil over as you throw it.

3 Continue in this way until you reach the other end of the plot. If you have any rotted manure or garden compost to incorporate, it should be placed at the base of each trench before it is filled in. Annual weeds can be buried, but perennial weed roots should be removed.

4 Once the last trench has been dug, fill it in with the soil from the first trench that has been barrowed to the end of the plot. Leave the soil surface rough; repeated freezing and thawing of the moisture in the soil over the winter will break down the clods and improve soil structure.

mid-winter

This is often the most trying season of the year for gardeners. The weather may be at its most miserable and, although the shortest day is just past, there is no real evidence yet of the daylight hours lengthening. Spring might seem a long way off but in reality there is not too long to wait.

All the dormant-season tasks in the garden continue. Planting bare-root specimens of new trees and shrubs will be possible for some weeks yet; if the weather is freezing or very wet when the plants arrive, heel them in until conditions improve. After heavy frosts, check plantings in case they need firming back into the soil if the frost has lifted them.

The prolonged wet spells show up any badly drained areas. If puddles are still standing on the soil surface hours after the rain has stopped, it is a sign drainage needs to be improved.

This is the most likely time for snow. Snow can make the garden look beautiful, but if you can bring yourself to spoil its unsullied whiteness it's a good idea to take action to prevent it from damaging plants and trees. It's only the physical weight of the snow that does the damage; snow actually helps to insulate plants against the cold.

Some border plants can be increased by root cuttings, and in the vegetable garden the soil can be made ready for early spring sowings. In the greenhouse things are moving ahead rapidly—stock up with the equipment you need for the busy sowing and growing season ahead.

◀ *Mid-winter is the most likely time for snow in many regions. It may be beautiful but its weight can cause damage to trees and plants.*

MIDWINTER TASKS

General
- Check and maintain tools before putting them away for the winter
- Improve drainage where necessary

Ornamental garden
- Weed and check emerging spring bulbs outdoors
- Take root cuttings of phlox, papaver (poppy), verbascum (mullein), and other border plants
- Continue planting bare-root and container-grown trees and shrubs, and refirm newly-planted specimens after frost. Heel in bare-root plants when weather is unsuitable for planting
- Knock snow off evergreens before it breaks their branches
- Order young plants from seed catalogs for delivery in early to mid-spring

▲ Root cuttings are an easy way to propagate many border plants.

Lawns
- Keep off the grass in frosty or wet weather
- Watch out for snow mould disease
- Sweep away leaves and debris

Kitchen garden
- Continue digging
- Force outdoor rhubarb for an early crop
- Sow sprouting seeds for winter salads
- Order vegetable seeds, seed potatoes, young vegetable plants, and onion sets from catalogs as soon as possible
- Sow beans and peas for an early crop
- Continue to check fruit and vegetables in store
- Cover the ground with cloches to dry it out ready for early sowings
- Continue to plant fruit trees, and soft fruit bushes and canes
- Complete pruning of fruit trees
- Deter birds from attacking fruit buds

▼ Grow a quick and early crop of carrots in a growing bag in the greenhouse.

Greenhouse
- Remove dead plant material promptly to avoid disease. Ventilate whenever possible to keep the atmosphere dry
- Buy new seed flats, pots, propagator tops, and labels, etc., ready for the main sowing season
- Continue sowing early seeds in a heated propagator
- Start overwintering fuchsias and pelargoniums, chrysanthemums and dahlias into growth to provide cuttings
- Sow Lathyrys odoratus (sweet peas)
- Sow some stump-rooted carrots and radishes in a growing bag

plants in season

Evergreen plants continue to give good value, especially the variegated varieties that light up the garden in dull weather. Many of the trees and shrubs flowering now have the bonus of an intense fragrance, and more and more bulbs are blooming.

▼ *Winter-flowering hellebores bring life to the garden. Although they are frost-hardy, low-growing varieties need protection.*

PERENNIALS

Ajuga reptans (bugle)

Bergenia

Helleborus atrorubens, H. foetidus (stinking hellebore), *H. niger* (Christmas rose)

Iris unguicularis

Phormium tenax (New Zealand flax)

Viola (winter-flowering pansies)

BULBS

Crocus ancyrensis, C. imperati, C. laevigatus, C. tomasinianus

Eranthis (winter aconite)

Galanthus (snowdrop)

Iris danfordiae, I. histrioides, I. reticulata (below)

TREES AND SHRUBS

Acer (bark effects) (maple)

Aucuba japonica (spotted laurel)

Betula (birch)

Camellia

Chimonanthus praecox (wintersweet)

Cornus alba (red-barked dogwood)

Corylus avellana 'Contorta' (Harry Lauder's walking stick)

Cotoneaster

Daphne odora

Erica carnea (alpine heath)

Euonymus fortunei, E. japonicus (variegated varieties) (spindle tree)

Garrya elliptica

Hamamelis mollis (witch hazel)

Hedera colchica 'Dentata Variegata' and others (ivy)

Hippophae rhamnoides (sea buckthorn)

Ilex (berry-bearing and variegated varieties) (holly)

Jasminum nudiflorum (jasmine)

Lonicera fragrantissima, L. standishii (winter honeysuckle)

Mahonia

Prunus serrula, P. × subhirtella 'Autumnalis' (fall cherry)

Pyracantha (firethorn)

Salix alba (white willow), *S. babylonica* var. *pekinensis* 'Tortuosa' (dragon-claw willow)

Skimmia japonica

Sorbus

Viburnum

▲ *Pyracantha, with its startling red berries, will liven up any garden at this time of year.*

◄ Camellia × williamsii *'Jury's yellow'* is a winter-flowering delight.

protecting fruit and sowing seeds

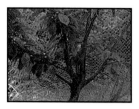

Plant canes and bushes to extend your range of soft fruits, and take action against birds that destroy fruit buds before they even start into growth. Cloches help to get the soil ready for early sowings, but if you can't wait that long, grow your own salad in a jelly jar in a matter of days.

Protecting fruit buds from birds

Various species of small birds can ruin the potential fruit crop of trees and bushes by pecking at the buds on the dormant branches. Every climate zone and local regions have their particular culprits, even including squirrels. Apples, cherries, gooseberries, plums, pears, and currants can all be affected.

The birds usually eat the tender shoots right in the center of the buds. It is also believed that sometimes the birds are searching for insects sheltering in and around the buds, and that the damage to the buds is incidental. Either way, the effect is the same: long lengths of branches and shoots are left bare and the fruit crop is reduced.

Bitter-tasting bird repellents can be sprayed on the trees but may not be very effective, while bird scarers also give mixed results. The surest way to prevent damage is by providing a physical barrier with netting or horticultural blanket.

BUSHES, CANES, AND FRUIT TREES

Fruit and vegetables form an important part of a healthy diet, and having plenty of home-grown fruit to harvest will certainly enable you to increase your consumption. Spells of good weather will allow you to plant fruit trees and soft fruit canes and bushes now.

Extend your range of soft fruits by trying some of the new, improved varieties that find their way into the catalogs every year. Particularly popular are the hybrid berries (mainly raspberry/blackberry crosses) such as boysenberry, silvanberry, tayberry, youngberry, sunberry, and veitchberry. They should provide a talking point and a good crop of tasty fruit.

▶ *Netting protects a fruit crop from birds, but earlier in the year it can also help to prevent them from destroying the developing buds.*

sprouting seeds for winter salads

Winter is a difficult time to produce fresh salad crops, but sprouting seeds couldn't be simpler to grow. They are ready in a matter or days, and have a pleasant crunchy texture and a range of interesting flavors. Many varieties are also thought to be beneficial to health, with particularly high concentrations of cancer-preventing compounds. A good range of suitable seeds for sprouting are available from the mail order catalogs of major seed merchants.

1 Sprouting seeds can be grown in a wide-necked glass jar topped with a piece of muslin or fine mesh net secured with an elastic band. A square cut from an old pair of nylon pantyhose makes a good cover.

2 Put a couple of spoonfuls of seeds into the jar and cover them with water; allow them to soak for a few hours or overnight (right). Drain the water off through the top of the jar, fill with fresh water, swirl around the jar and immediately drain the water off again.

3 Place the jar of seeds in a moderately warm position. If they are grown in the dark the sprouts will be white; if they are in the light they will be green and have a slightly different flavor. Every day, fill the jar with fresh water, swirl it round and immediately drain it away.

4 After a few days the sprouts are ready to eat (below); they will bulk up to almost fill the jar. Among seeds that can be grown are mung beans, alfalfa, and fenugreek; mixtures are also available. Only buy seeds produced for sprouting as many pulses are poisonous if eaten raw.

THE VEGETABLE PLOT

In a sheltered place in the vegetable garden, cover an area of ground with cloches to get it ready for seed sowing a little later. Although the cloches might help to trap what heat there is, this is not why they are useful. Their main purpose is to keep the rain off the soil so that it can dry out, enabling it to be broken down to the fine crumbs necessary to form a seedbed.

late winter

Although the weather can be terrible, there is no longer any doubt that spring is on its way. The days are lengthening; buds on the branches of trees and shrubs begin to swell, and more and more early bulbs are producing their flowers. Get those dormant-season tasks finished as soon as you can.

If jobs such as winter digging, planting bare-root trees and shrubs, and pruning fruit trees are not yet finished, this is the time to complete them. In most areas roses can safely be pruned now, too.

A few dry, breezy days will help to get the soil in good condition for sowing to take place outdoors shortly. If you do not know what type of soil you have, this is a good time to carry out tests.

Flower borders should be tidied, removing weeds and debris that shelter slugs and snails. This is particularly important because the tender young shoots of plants newly emerged through the soil are very vulnerable to these pests.

Mulching is equally important because it helps prevent further weed growth, keeps some of the moisture in the soil ready for drier weather, and makes the garden look much tidier and more attractive generally.

In the greenhouse there are increasing numbers of seeds to be sown and cuttings to be taken. It's vital to insure that the greenhouse heater is properly maintained and adjusted. It will still be needed for some time yet—there will soon be dozens of tender young seedlings that need wamth to develop. Seedlings from earlier sowings need pricking off, and space in the greenhouse will soon be at a premium.

In the kitchen garden, winter crops such as leeks and parsnips need to be used up before they start into growth again, and if you have forced rhubarb and kale for early crops you should harvest them now.

◀ *Now is the time to tidy up your flower borders because any slugs and snails sheltering in weeds and debris will attack young shoots.*

LATE WINTER TASKS

General

- Check tools and equipment, and buy new replacements if needed
- Carry out soil tests on various sites around the garden

▲ Add moisture-retaining compost to the bottom of the pole bean trench.

Ornamental garden

- Weed and clear borders, and mulch with bark
- Prune roses
- Finish planting bare-root trees and shrubs
- Weed overwintered hardy annuals and provide supports as necessary

- Protect vulnerable plants from slugs
- Sow Lathyrus odoratus (sweet peas) outside
- Continue to plant lily bulbs as available
- Prune winter jasmine after flowering

- Prune summer-flowering clematis hybrids
- Feed flowering shrubs with sulphate of potash

Lawns

- Mow the grass lightly if necessary. Carry out repairs to edges and aerate compacted areas
- Choose a new lawn mower if one is needed, before the main mowing season starts

Kitchen garden

- Use up winter vegetables such as leeks and parsnips from the garden before they regrow
- Complete winter digging and apply lime if necessary
- Prepare seed beds if the weather allows
- Use blanket, cloche, etc., to protect pea and bean seedlings, and spring greens

- Set seed potatoes to chit (sprout) in a light place as soon as they are purchased
- Plant shallots and Jerusalem artichokes
- Prepare a pole bean trench with moisture-retaining compost
- Harvest forced kale and rhubarb as soon as the shoots are large enough

- Prune fall-fruiting raspberries
- Feed fruit trees and bushes with high-potash fertilizer

Greenhouse

- Clean up the greenhouse to prepare for the new season
- Feed forced bulbs that have finished flowering, ready for planting in the garden later
- Take cuttings from chrysanthemums, dahlias, fuchsias, and pelargoniums

- Begin sowing tomatoes, melons, and cucumbers for greenhouse cropping. Sow half-hardy annuals and beans in pots for planting out later. Prick off seedlings sown earlier

- Start begonia tubers into growth
- Bring potted strawberries into the greenhouse for early crops
- Increase ventilation during the day in suitable weather

▲ Sow bush or fava beans in pots ready for planting outdoors later.

plants in season

The number of flowers blooming in the garden increases rapidly during this time as the winter slowly but surely moves toward spring. Catkins on bare branches elongate and become more prominent, and some of the earliest flowering cherries give a foretaste of the pleasures to come in the months ahead as the days begin to lengthen and the light returns.

▲ Prunus subhirtella *'Pendula Rubra'* offers
a stunning display during the late winter.

▲ Hamamelis intermedia 'Westerstede', with its delicate yellow blooms, adds color to winter.

▶ Mahonia aquifolium 'Smaragd' supplies rich shapes and textures to the garden.

TREES AND SHRUBS

Acacia dealbata (acacia)
Camellia
Chaenomeles japonica (Japanese quince)
Chimonanthus praecox (wintersweet)
Cornus alba (red-barked dogwood), *C. mas*
   (cornelian cherry)
Daphne odora, D. mezereum
Erica carnea
Garrya elliptica
Hamamelis (witch hazel)
Hedera colchica 'Dentata Variegata' and others
Jasminum nudiflorum (winter jasmine)
Lonicera fragrantissima, L. standishii (winter
   honeysuckle)
Magnolia campbellii
Mahonia × *media* 'Charity' and others
Prunus incisa 'February Pink' (Fuji cherry),
   P. mume (Japanese apricot), and others
Pyracantha (firethorn)
Salix alba (white willow), *S. babylonica* var.
   pekinensis 'Tortuosa' (dragon-claw willow)
Sarcococca hookeriana, S. humilis (Christmas box)
Skimmia
Sorbus
Stachyurus praecox
Viburnum

PERENNIALS

Bergenia
Helleborus niger (Christmas rose), *H. orientalis*
   (Lenten rose)
Phormium tenax (New Zealand flax)
Primula (primrose)
Pulmonaria (lungwort)
Viola odorata (English violet)

BULBS

Anemone blanda
Chionodoxa (glory of the snow)
Crocus
Cyclamen coum
Eranthis hyemalis (winter aconite)
Galanthus (snowdrop)
Iris danfordiae, I. histrioides, I. reticulata
Narcissus (daffodil)

◀ Daphne mezereum 'Rubra' is a delight in the garden at this time of year.

protecting and planting

Dry, breezy days at this time of year will dry out the soil and allow seedbeds to be prepared shortly, but if the weather should turn windy and cold, young crops may need some protection. Jerusalem artichokes are a very easy crop to grow, and the tubers can be planted now.

Protecting seedlings

This is still an unpredictable time of year as far as the weather goes—it can produce some of the coldest conditions of the winter, often after a mild spell has already started plants into growth.

The young plants of beans and peas that were sown in the fall can be given a severe set-back by poor weather now, but they can be protected from the worst of it with cloches or lengths of lightweight horticultural blanket.

Spring cabbage plants not planted out in the fall can be set out in their cropping positions when the weather is suitable. Like the pea and bean seedlings, they can be protected with cloches or blanket if conditions deteriorate after they are planted.

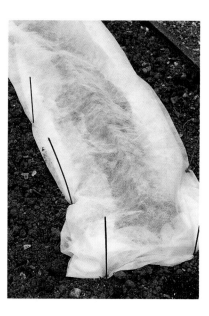

▼ *At this time of year it may be a good idea to use a blanket (or cloche) to protect pea and bean seedlings against harsh weather.*

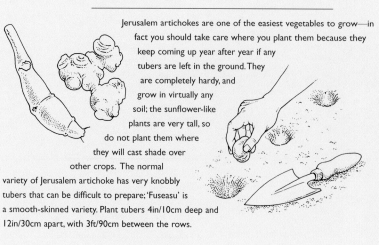

PLANTING JERUSALEM ARTICHOKES

Jerusalem artichokes are one of the easiest vegetables to grow—in fact you should take care where you plant them because they keep coming up year after year if any tubers are left in the ground. They are completely hardy, and grow in virtually any soil; the sunflower-like plants are very tall, so do not plant them where they will cast shade over other crops. The normal variety of Jerusalem artichoke has very knobbly tubers that can be difficult to prepare; 'Fuseasu' is a smooth-skinned variety. Plant tubers 4in/10cm deep and 12in/30cm apart, with 3ft/90cm between the rows.

prepare for pole beans

Pole beans are one of the most worthwhile crops for gardeners. They produce a very large crop in relation to the space they occupy, and have an extended season throughout the summer, right up until the first frosts. Although it is a little too early to think about raising the plants yet, it is not too soon to start preparing the soil where they are to grow.

KALE AND RHUBARB

Stems of kale (pictured below) and rhubarb that have been forced into early growth in a frost-free greenhouse should be ready for cutting now. The shoots should have been kept completely dark by covering them with a black bucket or container—this gives the most tender results and prevents kale from becoming bitter. Kale is an unusual luxury vegetable (not to be confused with kale beet, which is quite different). It is often compared to asparagus, but the creamy white stems have a flavor all of their own.

1 Choose a warm, sheltered site for pole beans, preferably moving them to a new position each year to avoid root-rotting fungi building up in the soil. Dig a trench at least one spit deep—more if you can manage it—and 2ft/60cm or so wide. Fork over the soil in the bottom of the trench to break it up (right).

2 Beans need fertile and, above all, moisture-retentive soil. Adequate levels of soil moisture are necessary to insure reliable setting of the flowers (flowers often drop off unfertilized in dry conditions, leading to poor crops), and rapid development of tender, juicy pods.

3 Add a layer of moisture-retentive material to the base of the trench. Ideally this should be well-rotted manure containing plenty of straw (below), but a mix of materials such as grass clippings, spent hops, spent mushroom compost, and even old newspapers can be used.

4 Leave the trench open to the rain until it is time for sowing or planting the beans after the last frosts in the spring. Then make sure the base of the trench is thoroughly soaked, by watering if necessary, before returning the topsoil and treading it thoroughly to firm.

crop rotation

It is not good practice to grow the same crops in the same places in the vegetable garden year after year. There are several reasons for this.

Different crops have slightly different nutrient requirements. Brassicas, for instance, are known as greedy crops (or gross feeders) because they take a high level of nutrients, particularly nitrogen, from the soil. If brassicas are grown on the same piece of ground year in, year out, the nutrients in the soil could soon be exhausted, particularly if no organic matter or fertilizers are added to replace them. Brassicas are also prone to certain specific pests and diseases, such as clubroot; these can persist in the soil, or on crop remains, ready to infect the new crop the following year.

If a different crop is grown in the brassicas' plot next year, however, it is likely to take different types of nutrients from the soil. It will also be immune to brassica-specific pests and diseases, so that the cycle of infection can be broken. This practice of insuring that different types of crop are grown in succeeding years on the same piece of ground is known as crop rotation. Deciding exactly which crop should be grown where obviously needs careful planning. There are various crop rotation schemes, but a common one is to divide the types of crops that are grown into three main groups.

Dividing the crops

The first group is the brassicas—cabbages of all types, Brussels sprouts, kale, broccoli, cauliflower, and so on. They have a high nitrogen requirement, and are prone to clubroot disease. The second group is root crops—potatoes, parsnips, carrots, beets, Jerusalem artichokes, salsify and scorzonera, and so on. They have a slightly lower nitrogen requirement, and are likely to be misshapen if fresh manure has been added to the soil recently. Finally there are peas and beans—these are unusual because they obtain nitrogen from the air rather than the soil. Because of nitrogen-fixing bacteria that live

▲ Cauliflowers fall into the brassicas group of vegetables. This group is known as "greedy crops" because they need a high level of soil nutrients.

▲ Peas belong to a group of plants that actually add nitrogen to the soil, and so replace the nutrients used by brassicas the previous year.

▲ *Carrots belong to the root crop group,*
alongside potatoes, parsnips, beets,
and Jerusalem artichokes.

CROP ROTATION

	Bed A	Bed B	Bed C
Year 1	*Brassicas*	*Roots*	*Peas and beans*
Year 2	*Peas and beans*	*Brassicas*	*Roots*
Year 3	*Roots*	*Peas and beans*	*Brassicas*
Year 4	*Brassicas*	*Roots*	*Peas and beans*

SIZE MATTERS

There is one major difficulty with a rotation, and that is the need for each of the three groups to occupy exactly the same amount of space. The imaginative use of miscellaneous crops (such as lettuce, squash, spinach, and so on) can help here because they can be placed in any of the three groups, as necessary, to balance things out. However, the rotation does not have to be followed slavishly—it will have to be adjusted for practical purposes.

on their roots they will actually add to the amount of nitrogen in the soil.

Of course, not all crops fall neatly into these three groups. Crops such as rutabaga and turnips are both brassicas and root crops, so which group would they go in? And what about spinach, or squash and zucchini, or onions? Rutabaga, turnips, and kohlrabi are included in the brassica group, mainly because they can be infected by clubroot disease. Since spinach is a hungry crop with a high nitrogen requirement it also fits well into the brassicas. Most other crops such as lettuces, tomatoes, squash, leeks, onions and so on are generally included with the peas and beans, simply because they are neither brassicas nor true root crops. However, there are no hard and fast rules about these miscellaneous crops, and onions are sometimes included with the root crops, while spinach joins the peas and beans, for example.

Establishing the rotation

The vegetable plot is divided into three and each of these three main groups of crops is grown in their own section—for example, brassicas in Bed A, root crops in Bed B, and peas and beans in Bed C. Next year, peas and beans move into Bed A, brassicas into Bed B, and roots into Bed C. The following year they all move round one place again, and the year after that they are back where they started.

This means that the bed with roots can be manured at the end of the season ready for the brassicas, and the roots follow the peas and beans that have added nitrogen to the soil to make up for the absence of manure.

Four- or five-bed rotations are also possible by splitting the groups up further, but they become increasingly complicated. The three-bed scheme is the most practical for the majority of gardens.

index

PICTURE CREDITS:
Liz Eddison/Designers: Aughton Green Landscapes, Tatton Park 2001, 49b; Bill Cartlidge, Tatton Park 2000, 22; Julian Dowle lff; Paul Dyer, Chelsea 2001, 48br; Carol Klein, 32; Land Art, Hampton Court 2000, c; Angela Mainwaring, Hampton Park 2001, 30; Tom Stuart-Smith, Chelsea 2000, 10b; Neil Holmes: fc, 58bl; 61t, b; 67t; 86. Harry Smith Collection: fcb, b46, 62, 84, 91bl; Illustrator: Coral Mula bc.